ZERO TO HERO

ZERO TO HERO

"*Zero to Hero* is a heartfelt exploration of what it means to grow, lead, and remain human throughout it all. In the chapter, "The Leadership Journey," Nora Osman distills years of experience into lessons that feel both hard-earned and hopeful. Her writing reminds us that authentic leadership isn't about perfection—it's about courage, curiosity, and compassion in motion.

—JEFF TON, Former CIO, Author, Speaker, and Fellow at the Institute for Digital Transformation

"*Zero to Hero* speaks to the moments that shape us long before we ever have language for them. Nora Osman captures the reality of leadership not as a formula, but as a deeply human journey marked by disruption, reflection, and resilience. Through honest storytelling, the book honors the 'gut punch' moments that force us to reckon with who we are, what we value, and how we choose to move forward. It is a reminder that transformation does not begin with strategy, but with experience."

—KATHRYN LANCIONI, Fellow with the Institute for Digital Transformation, ICF-certified Leadership Coach, and Host of the Gut Punch podcast

"*Zero to Hero: The Human Experience in Leadership & Business Transformation* is an open, honest, and deeply personal exploration of how to cultivate a true 'Hero' mindset throughout your life's journey. It illustrates how embracing your mistakes, moving forward with purpose, and striving to become your authentic self can positively influence the people around you in meaningful and lasting ways.

I highly recommend not only reading this book but also taking notes as you go, so you can fully absorb and apply the powerful insights Nora shares from her own experiences."

—PETE MCGARAHAN, Founder/Principal Consultant McGarahan & Associates, Inc.

"*Zero to Hero* has real tribulations and crucibles—it is truly interesting, conscious, and clearly comes from the heart. It felt natural and meant to be."

—AMIR STERNHELL, Chief Strategy Officer at Sertainty Corporation

Zero to Hero

THE HUMAN EXPERIENCE IN LEADERSHIP
AND BUSINESS TRANSFORMATION

NORA M. OSMAN

LUMINARE PRESS

WWW.LUMINAREPRESS.COM

Luminare Press
442 Charnelton St.
Eugene, OR 97401
www.luminarepress.com

LCCN: 2026901086
ISBN: 979-8-90071-073-0

For my mother and father,
who taught me what humanity truly means.

For my husband,
who has walked beside me through every chapter of life.

For my children,
who are the purpose and pride of my life.

For my family,
who remind me every day of the power
of presence, purpose, and love.

And for every human
trying to make their moments count.

CONTENTS

PART 1

Ignition: Mindset and First Leaps

PART 2

People First: Becoming the Leader Others Choose to Follow

PART 3

Experience by Design: HX to CX in the Real World

PART 4

Transformation: Vision, Faith, and the Ongoing Shift

FOREWORD

Leadership isn't a destination—it's a lifelong expedition. Some days, it feels like discovery, others, like survival. What matters most is how we respond in those moments of truth, the ones that ask us to listen more deeply, to choose courage over comfort, and to keep showing up when the path ahead is uncertain.

That's what *Zero to Hero: The Human Experience in Leadership and Business Transformation* is really about. Nora Osman doesn't hand us a list of leadership tips or tidy formulas. She offers something far more valuable—her story. In these pages, she invites us to walk alongside her as she navigates the messy, beautiful, and deeply human terrain of leading and living with purpose.

From the very first chapter, Nora reminds us that transformation doesn't arrive as a single flash of brilliance—it happens through hundreds of small decisions. It's in the moments when we say yes before we feel ready, when we ask questions instead of pretending to know the answers, when we dare to believe there's more in us than the world expects to see. *Zero to Hero* is an invitation to notice those moments, to learn from them, and to lead with intention.

I was especially moved by the chapter "The Leadership Journey." It captures what so few leadership books ever do: the interior life of a leader. The doubt. The wonder. The tension between wanting to serve and needing to grow. Nora doesn't write from a podium— she writes from the trenches, where authentic leadership lives. She shows how trust is built one conversation at a time, how courage often begins as quiet persistence, and how humility turns mistakes into milestones.

Reading this chapter, I found myself reflecting on my own journey—the mentors who believed in me before I believed in myself, the teams that taught me more than I ever taught them, and the moments that demanded not authority, but authenticity. Nora captures that paradox perfectly: that leadership asks us to be both strong and vulnerable, both visionary and grounded.

What makes her voice so compelling is its honesty. She doesn't pretend to have it all figured out, and that's precisely why her lessons land. You can feel her curiosity and compassion in every story. You can sense the gratitude she carries for those who guided her and the responsibility she feels to guide others in return.

In a world that often confuses visibility with value, *Zero to Hero* brings us back to what truly matters—people. The human experience is the foundation of leadership, not an afterthought. Our teams, our families, our communities—they don't need perfect leaders; they need present ones. They need leaders willing to ask the hard questions, to listen without judgment, and to create spaces where others can thrive.

Nora Osman's work reminds us that leadership is not a title bestowed but a trust earned. It's a journey that begins the moment we choose to take responsibility for something beyond ourselves and continues as long as we continue to learn.

If you've ever doubted whether your story matters or wondered if your hard-won lessons have purpose, this book will remind you that they do. *Zero to Hero* isn't just about becoming a better leader; it's about becoming a fuller human being.

So take your time with these pages. Reflect on your own moments of truth. Let Nora's stories challenge you, comfort you, and call you forward. Because, as she so clearly shows, the journey of leadership is never about reaching the summit; it's about who we become along the way.

—Jeffrey S. Ton
Author of *Amplify Your Value, Amplify Your Job Search,*
and *Uncharted Moments*

PROLOGUE

There's no place better to start than the beginning. This book is about the journey of transformation, specifically mine. It's written with the intention of sharing stories: the different stops along the way that shaped me, the lessons learned, the pitfalls I stumbled into, and the triumphs that lifted me higher than I thought possible.

I was born in Brooklyn, New York, but my childhood took an unexpected turn when my parents plucked me from the city and moved us across continents. Because of my father's work, we lived in different parts of the world, which meant I spent first through ninth grade in international schools. There, I was surrounded by classmates from every corner of the globe, taught by strict British teachers, and immersed in cultures that made diversity feel natural, not exceptional. I didn't know "race" or "religion" as dividing lines, just people, each with their own stories, accents, and ways of being. It was an education in humanity before I ever stepped into a classroom in the US.

Books were my constant companions. I'd read through the night, flashlight in hand, devouring story after story. As the eldest of four children, I shouldered extra responsibilities, which pushed me to grow up faster than many of my peers. I also discovered my love for music and art, and, if I'm honest, a deep obsession with order and organization, bordering on OCD. These threads, curiosity, responsibility, creativity, and a hunger for knowledge, became the foundation of who I am.

When I returned to the US as a high school sophomore, it was like a cultural crash course. I landed in an advanced Long Island school system where competition was fierce, hormones were raging, and suddenly the world wasn't as seamless as my international upbringing had suggested. For the first time, I became aware of the divides—racial, cultural, socioeconomic—that shaped how people treated each other. That realization stayed with me.

In college, I started down the path of medicine, my father's dream for me. Back then, "success" was defined in narrow titles: doctor, lawyer, engineer. A year and a half into pre-med, I realized it wasn't my dream at all. I pivoted, completing a dual degree in business management and French (which I'd studied for nearly a decade). That decision set me on the winding path you'll read about in these pages.

I married young, became a mother early, and built a career at the same time. It wasn't easy—but it was real. And it was full of the kinds of moments I now call zero-to-hero: ordinary circumstances where an unexpected decision, a hard truth, or an uncomfortable leap transformed everything.

This is my story. Written by me, not a ghostwriter, and definitely not AI. But more importantly, it's an invitation: to see yourself in these pages, to remember your own moments of truth, and to discover how ordinary people—you, me, all of us—are capable of extraordinary things.

PART 1

Ignition: Mindset and First Leaps

CHAPTER 1

The Zero to Hero Mindset

I've always been fascinated by people, the way they think, sound, move, and show up. They're the heroes of their own stories, and maybe even ours. That's why I, among many of us, always loved watching movies as a child, and still do as an adult. We watch movies to step into an alternative reality, to transform (if even temporarily) into a different world, where things that were seemingly impossible become possible. And one of the things I am fascinated with is the idea of a plain, common person becoming a hero. What is especially unique about this is the idea of an unlikely situation arising, presenting an opportunity for this common person to step into a situation, doing something unique and powerful. The unexpected becomes reality, and the person stepping into a power they didn't know they had is what's fascinating to me. But from that standpoint, it's something we're *all* capable of doing but aren't always aware of. No one is born a hero—they become a hero in an instant when they choose discomfort over comfort—the unfamiliar and the unknown over the routine and safe path of life. So why am I talking about this area right now? Because I'm planting a seed, that we each have the ability to go from zero to hero in an instant! And I challenge that in most of our days, we opt for the safe route, we keep things simple and quiet and comfortable … until something jarring happens.

This book is going to be real and raw. It's not going to sugarcoat anything, just share the truth of the ups and downs of the journey I embarked on decades ago, long before I came to realize it would be a journey. I'm that common person who never felt she was special in any unique way. I wasn't born with a super special gift, and I still don't believe I have any unique talent that hasn't been heard of. But what I've come to realize is that the combination of the mindset I have, as well as the experiences that I've gone through, has set the tone for how I see the world, the lens with which I evaluate everything, and then how I choose to take action. You'll hear many stories of those moments when there was great doubt, great fear, and even great disdain. We all go through those experiences, and it's up to us to either choose to see them as lessons to learn from or as things we'd rather suppress and forget. But what I've come to realize most is that you can't erase the past, and you can't deny your experiences. You can try, but the more you do, the more it will feel like you're trying to submerge a balloon into deep waters. You just can't hold it down too long—the air within it will keep it floating. You're best letting it go, letting it float away behind you. Let the waves of the water carry it somewhere that you don't need to worry about. You know it's there, you can acknowledge it was there, but you don't have to keep looking at it or trying to bury it.

One of my favorite expressions is "mistakes refine you, they don't define you." I love this because it comes back to the idea that we're all a work in progress, we're never truly done. If we see ourselves as in a state of continuous evolution and improvement, we evolve. We're never fully *done done*. We may be done with a task or achieve a specific goal or milestone, but that's not the end. So long as we also embrace our mistakes as lessons that we need, we continue to grow and evolve. I'll be sharing a lot of these mistakes, the bricks that hit my head, the wakeup moments, the embarrassing ones, the goofy ones, and ones that I would've loved to have buried deep in the ocean, but just like that balloon, I know it would just surface again. So, I'm letting it go and letting it float away behind me. And by sharing, I aim to help you see that you too are capable of achieving more than you ever thought possible. You are the seed, you have all that you need within you. All you need is to be nurtured in the right way—the right soil for your roots, the right light and temperature to warm up, and water in the right increments. All you need is to be loved, and this starts with loving yourself, understanding yourself, and forgiving yourself when you do things you regret, or you fail in ways you wished you hadn't. Remember, heroes weren't born that way, they evolved. They chose a path, they failed along the way, they had good days and many bad ones. They chose to "do what's right, and not what's easy. What's easy isn't always right, and what's right isn't always easy" (a favorite saying I started sharing decades ago).

CHAPTER 2

The Transformation... Starting with Three Pivots

So here it goes. Three stories, three pivotal moments, and saying yes.

Pivot One: Curiosity over Comfort

I remember the first time I stepped out of my comfort zone. The first time I got asked to try something totally out of my job description and I said yes. I was working at a commercial insurance company out on Long Island, close to my first residence. My role right out of college was a basic accounting clerk. I quickly learned all there was to learn about keying in accounts receivable entries and then accounts payable entries. They even had me try my talent at collections (which wasn't fun at all, but necessary). What I didn't anticipate ever doing was anything with technology. The controller at the company was a friendly man with an outgoing personality. He enjoyed poking his head around, checking in with the team. He asked a lot of questions, and many on the personal side. In little to no time, he learned that I had a curious mind as well. One day, he stopped by and asked me, "How'd you like to learn a little bit about the commands in DOS?" At that moment, I had no idea what DOS was or why I would want to learn about it, but, being that curious body, I said sure, why not. He started up a DOS prompt, and the intimidating black screen with a blinking green character waiting was the beginning of a series of short lessons. He taught me how to list a directory, make a directory, and move files around. I didn't quite know the point of doing all that, but I couldn't help but feel excited about knowing something that most didn't. It was almost like a little secret. The controller, I'll refer to him as "M," would check in on me from time to time to see how I was doing with the lesson and if I'd tried anything fun. And that was all I needed by way of invitation to explore. Clearly, this was a safe zone, and I was given the license to poke around, so why not use it? And that's precisely what I did.

One day, while waiting for a batch of records to update on the mainframe, I decided to take a close look at the DOS folder structure. I couldn't quite understand why the files were all jumbled together. There were .exe files, .bat files, and .com files. In my infinite wisdom, I decided to make top-level folders and move all like files under them. Yep, all the .exe files together, all the .bat files together, and all the .com files together. I think I even made an "Other" folder and moved anything that didn't match those three. And then reality hit. Nothing worked on that system from that point on. I couldn't quite understand why. So, as M stopped in that day to check, I shared with him my dilemma, and he asked, "You did what?" and then chuckled for a good thirty seconds straight. And that was the first big lesson I learned from M. He said to me, "Just because you can, doesn't mean you should." That was after sharing that I'd essentially attempted to rearrange the program that runs the computer, which completely made it inoperable, as it was designed to work in a specific sequence, with each file referencing a different file, in a specific location. My OCD and pure ignorance taught me that first, tough lesson.

 **If you don't know, you should ask.** That doesn't mean you don't try things out; you can do that, but with safety and caution

always, and always know when to ask for help, or do the research and learn proactively.

The good news that came from this exercise was that I'd essentially shown a key characteristic that leaders look for in their prodigies—curiosity. And from then on, I was offered the opportunity to help out with tasks supporting the mainframe, which led to a supporting role in IT, learning personal computers and terminal emulation to connect to the mainframe, and eventually to learning how to support a network, adding on workstations to connect. Showing curiosity and a desire to learn was a very big deal for me. It signaled the ability to step outside of my comfort zone, to be vulnerable, to do more. I eventually got promoted to manager of IT, and by the time I'd left that first company, I was managing the entire IT stack, including the mainframe, the network, the PCs, and all the applications on them.

Pivot Two: Brotherhood and Belonging

I also remember the first moment I felt the total pressure of leaving the safety of my cocoon—accepting a role in a very large, global software company based in New York. Although its headquarters was on Long Island, the main office I'd be supporting and working out of was Midtown New York City. New York City—that big, scary metropolitan city that we watch on TV, where people may get lost or feel unsafe. While I longed for safety and the comfort of a simple routine, I also yearned for excitement. I said yes to what truly scared me—the unknown. Still young, in my twenties, and also mom of a toddler child by then, I couldn't help but wonder what that door would open. When I first started working, there was the exploration period, all the new things. The rides on the LIRR (Long Island Railroad) that took me into Penn Station and landed me at the same track most days, yet each exit went to a unique part of the block. I recall being completely puzzled by how that was. It took me four full days to recognize that there was the Seventh

Avenue side and the Eighth Avenue side, and that each car on the train had a position closer to one or the other (or just the middle), which factored into where I would end up on a street or avenue. Figuring out the map of the station and the immediate vicinity was an irritating task but a necessary one. Learning how to navigate a lunch hour, food venues within proximity and budget, all on a tight hour schedule, was another task. But all of these minor learnings paled in comparison to the massive lesson I learned when I got down to business. *Whatever you don't know, you can learn, and there are people there who want to teach you.*

In those first few months of working at this technology company, I had by far the largest growth spurt on the technical side. I learned from my peers who had more exposure to operating systems and software applications than I had. They taught me about databases, virus software, remote control systems, and how to back up/restore systems. They spent hours showing me around the shortcuts I needed to master and helped me gain proficiency in what was a very short period. Back then, my role was that of a systems engineer, so I needed to be technically proficient enough to demonstrate enterprise management software solutions and be the right-hand guy (or gal) to the account executive (sales rep) there. What I loved the most about this experience is the brotherhood I found. Being surrounded by super smart people, young and more mature, who had no ego but had mastery and a spirit of giving, was priceless. It was intoxicating to be within that team, to learn at a rapid rate, and to shine among the giants. I recall feeling the excitement with every opportunity to present/demonstrate a solution in front of a leadership audience. Every time I had prepared and done the work to ready the system (and myself) for the need, it paid off. I shared what I learned willingly, but what I enjoyed most was being with my peers and having a sense of teamwork; we each had an area of expertise, but we also had a mutual respect. We cheered each other on, we marketed one another's talents, and we celebrated everyone's success together.

Saying yes that second time landed me in the spotlight as a technical talent with a flair for communicating and presenting, which was applauded. Something worth mentioning, I was the only young woman in the midst of a pool of young men. I could've felt a heightened sense of insecurity, inadequacy, and inferiority all at once. But being in the midst of kind, generous spirits, feeling the warmth of the team spirit, that's what made all the difference. It could've ended very differently if I'd gone in with a defensive posture, closing myself off to the team, focusing on the difference in my gender and marital status. But leaning into what binds us more than what separates us allowed for the opportunity to be part of a great team and to gain great experience in that stretch of time.

And then something unique happened while I was in that role. I had advanced myself as a subject matter expert and had been traveling to multiple states attending conferences, presenting to clients, and getting more limelight while doing so. It was a very uplifting time. I had found my tribe and my purpose, or so I thought. Every six months, there was this annoyance of a reorg that would happen, causing there to be a reshuffle in management, landing my team and me under a different technical support sales manager. At one point, the manager we were with, well-liked and respected, spent time with each of us, deep diving into our career aspirations. That manager acknowledged my achievements and what I had to offer technically. While in a performance review, he then asked me if I could see myself at a fork in the road, with the right side of the road having me continuing as a technical subject matter expert (SME), with plenty of accolades coming my way, and the left side would be the management road, having me managing a team of people delivering service. My immediate reaction was to say I'm made for the right side of the road—the tried-and-true technical SME role I knew and enjoyed. I'd only been doing that for three years, loved my team, loved the company, so why would I want to change?

Within three months of that conversation, another reorg transpired, landing my team and me under yet another manager. This one was different—he walked a different walk, he talked a different talk, and he brought about a completely different type of energy, a negative energy like none I'd seen before. I'll refer to him as "Z-man." I learned some tough lessons while working for Z-man. I learned what toxic leadership looked, sounded, and felt like. I learned what belittling, condescending, and continuously demoralizing leadership could do to a team. In fact, I experienced it firsthand, with a pep talk that I'll share. While having my first one-on-one with Z-man, he told me to imagine a forest with tall pine trees, getting all the sun, the rain, and growing proud and tall … with little shrubs at the bottom of that same forest, living in the shadows of the pine trees. The words uttered next from his mouth shocked me. He said, "You're like a shrub, under those tall trees … not able to get the light, not able to grow." And that was it. In his eyes, I was a shrub! I'd seen myself as one of those tall pine trees for three years, so I had no idea how my image had suddenly shifted. And in the eyes of someone who had little to no knowledge or exposure to what I'd delivered, or even what I was capable of delivering, that was harsh. Hearing that was a low blow, with the potential of being a fatal blow. But being a fire sign, all it served to do was to fuel the fire, to boost me forward and out of that situation. I'd learned plenty of lessons up until then; some were technical, but many were around leadership. I had seen the best of leadership—the kind that asks the tough questions, challenges your limiting beliefs, and sees something in you that you may not see yourself. And I'd seen the worst of leadership—a myopic mindset, ego-driven, built on command and control, limiting people's value, and affecting their confidence. That was a big lesson to learn, and experiencing the toxic leadership style firsthand for that brief period was well worth the lesson I learned from it.

On the heels of that conversation, I decided to venture out into the unknown world of management for the first time. Door Number Two, the left side of the road, the one I'd said *absolutely not* to just a few months before, came into my purview. I knew that I was nowhere near ready for the road ahead. I had neither the experience nor the skill to manage a group of people. But what I knew was that saying yes the first two times had served me well, so I said yes, this third time, which made for the third pivot.

Pivot Three: The Manager I Wasn't Ready to Be (Yet)

This time, the pivot was different; it was venturing out from being a sole contributor to being one responsible for the contributions of others. It took me into truly uncharted territory. Up until then, I'd only known how to manage myself; organized, focused, self-disciplined, I was able to understand the assignments, work through them, and deliver exceptionally well. I knew what excellence looked like, and I was eager to please. But stepping into a space like this, with no guardrails, where other people's performance would reflect on my own, wow, that was a tall order and a huge risk. I reflect on the moment I went on the interview for the manager role of a help desk at a health care insurance company. It wasn't prescheduled; it basically just happened, midday while I was already in the city. I wore neither an interview suit nor had I seen a job description. It was just an "exploratory" meeting with the to-be hiring manager. I showed up in a lavender suit with a silk, floral blouse, armed with nothing but my personality and my presence. At the time, I was still working under Z-man, totally frustrated, deflated, and essentially confused. The last thing I thought I would be exploring was a management position. But you know what they say, desperate measures for desperate times. At the interview, it felt casual, friendly, and surprisingly comfortable. The questions I was asked were woven into a conversation, one that was enjoyable. It felt warm, exciting, and like someone had extended an arm out to me, saying, "Let's give this a try … I believe in you." And so I said yes to the road on the left, the unpaved, bumpy, uncharted road. And it was the single most catapulting change I made in my entire career up until that moment.

Saying yes to the unknown was once again saying yes to myself, showing that I believed in myself. In saying yes, when I knew I wasn't ready or prepared, meant I believed in myself. **Saying yes right then signaled that I put all my stock in myself, and that I was willing to take the chance, invest in myself, and wait for the returns, whenever they came.** That was the biggest lesson I learned. You're never really ready to step into a management or leadership role—but you may have the qualities to lead well earlier than you're ready. It takes a discerning, smart leader to see that in you and to extend a hand. I was fortunate enough to have this happen to me twice—once by the manager who asked me the question about the fork in the road, and the second time by the leader who took me on the journey that started with my first management position, when I was most uncertain. When I was least prepared. When I knew the stakes were highest, as by then I'd been married, had a mortgage, and was already mom to two kids under three years old. Despite craving easy, craving safety, I knew the only way to unlock what's truly awesome was to face my fears, to say yes when I was not ready, and to have faith. Having faith made all the difference. Leaning on the experiences of the past, of the first nine years of my career, and knowing that the rest is still unwritten would be plenty for me to work with.

Years later, I would mentor many young men and women, and I'd get asked how I got my start in IT and in leadership. I often told these same stories, not because they're inspiring but because they're real. Everyone has a unique story, a blueprint for their life and their journey. Mine is what it is. I'm grateful to have the instinct to keep saying "why not" to answer the question of "why." I've come to learn that it's not everyone's stance, in fact it's rare that you find people who keep challenging the status quo and looking for "different." I say different because at the time you say why not, you don't quite know if it's better, you just know it's different. And different can be all that you need to challenge yourself into a world of opportunity.

Sometimes I wonder if I had shied away from Mr. M at first, hadn't dabbled in computers when I got that chance, if my life and world would've been entirely different. My guess is absolutely it would've been. Perhaps I would've stayed in the pack, the one that worked thirty-plus years in the same company, took the same thirty-minute lunch break, and complained every Monday morning about how they hate Mondays. Maybe that would've been safe, but what I know for sure is it wouldn't have been anywhere as fulfilling as the journey I ended up on. The final thing I learned is *no*, and saying *no* may mean it leaves you with "no options" in the end because you keep closing doors that pry open, leaving you locked up in the same room and path that limits your growth, your opportunity, and stifles your spirit in the end.

CHAPTER 3

Managing to Lead

If you'd asked me if there was ever a scenario I could see where I'd be a manager of a help desk in New York and responsible for the performance results of the people on a daily basis, I would've said absolutely no way. Up until that first time I said yes to the manager role, I'd viewed managers as a necessary evil. We had to have them, they served a purpose, to herd the cattle (or cats) and keep everyone in check. I thought it must be a tedious job, one you had to be insane to want, and one that had few perks beyond a bigger desk and a bigger salary. I was never one who craved that kind of attention, the one where I would have authority over others from a hierarchical perspective. Sure, I was the oldest of four in my family, so naturally I knew a thing or two about setting the course for the others and modeling better behavior. That said, it wasn't my true intention to get into management, but it was my destiny.

I recall the first time I walked into the room where the staff sat, and I was introduced to each one of them briefly. Their names were in my head for a fleeting moment, but their facial expressions lingered in my memory. Why were they so apprehensive-looking? They didn't seem happy; they seemed tired, like they'd had some *really hard* days. I started hearing the word "helpless desk" when others would refer to this team, and I couldn't quite grasp how they had gotten there. My new manager, a director of technology operations, had greeted me a few days in with a yellow-lined note-pad paper with a list of things he needed me to be on top of, which I took as the requirements. Short of that, I had free rein to figure out how to manage the team.

The first thing that struck me was that everything was so loosely defined. How they managed support interactions was barely documented (the process) but could be explained in thirty seconds or less. How they interacted with other teams when assigning work, basic, with these teams feeling hopelessly underserved and ill-prepared to support the customers based on the little information provided or effort made to support those users on first contact with the help desk. Unfortunately, with every individual I interviewed from that team, I grew less certain that anyone had any grasp on what work they were delivering or how they delivered it. There were no metrics.

Lesson 1—You Can't Manage What You Don't Measure

Recognizing that they had some tools, like a ticketing system and an automated call distributor system where some data could be extracted, that was a start. Actually looking at what should be measured was progress. Having had exposure to applications that do a great job of contact management of support, such as the IT service management platform they were on and that I'd been familiar with in my prior role with the same vendor I'd been employed at, I got started. But I didn't assume that just because you know the tool, you know what the process should be or the data you need to manage it. That's when I decided to go do some learning. I looked for books on the basics of running a help desk and got started on my learning journey. This was good stuff—they explained the *what* to measure, when, and how. That was sufficient to provide a blueprint for how to get going, and since there was nothing there before this, anything I put in place was progress. I spent time with the most senior person on the team, a team lead, who quickly became a case study for me. He had been there for upward of fifteen years by that point, knew everyone and everything about the systems they were supporting, and was able to provide the types of insights I needed to validate steps.

In little time, I had a daily metrics report, measuring basics like volume, resolution percentages for the team, then by person, etc. Then I made these into weekly reports and eventually monthly reports. It was the beginning of defining a baseline, which was critical to understanding where the team was at. It also helped me understand how this team's work impacted other teams' activities. Clearly, the sister technology teams were not enamored with this team's performance, and for good reason, yet they had nothing to offer by way of ideas or support. They were simply expecting better, and it was up to me to figure out how to deliver that.

In addition to measuring transactions, I had the intuition that the more important part was to start to learn about the people on an individual level. You see, you can't make demands on people's performance until you understand who they are and what makes them tick. Their strengths, where they struggle, how they like to be addressed. In very little time, I'd interviewed each person, gotten to know much more than their name, title, length of time there. I knew more about their life, their ambitions to have families of their own, their hobbies, what they enjoyed about the work they did. Spending time with them and asking simple but deep questions made them feel heard. They loved that I cared to take them off the phones and get to know them, and that I truly had an open door (technically and figuratively, since it was an alcove office with a glass partition but no door).

Lesson 2—It Starts and Ends with People

The benefit of spending a good amount of time with the team members was not just getting to know them individually, it was hearing their ideas on what they needed and had not been given. It was easy for everyone to label them "helpless" and feel they had little value when they were never given any resources to work with. If all they were empowered to do was reset a password, it's no wonder the frustration levels were high. Among them were individuals with A-plus certifications, some experience with programming, and others who had done other roles like network administration or desktop support. Clearly, they were smart, capable people, but without the tools and attention needed for them to thrive.

From each person I spoke to, I compiled a list of needs; some said they wished they could have higher-level administrative rights, others wished they could physically visit end users so they could see what they were talking about, while others expressed the lack of training on the main systems they got calls for. I also decided to speak with members from other sister technology teams to get their perspective on what they wanted from level one and what was missing from the workflow that we could work on. While they were happy to share, I could see they were skeptical about my ability to deliver any of that. I knew as I heard from the varying team members that compiling the list wasn't enough; I had to deliver some of what they needed to maintain credibility. That's when I realized what work was ahead—significant.

Lesson 3—Making Stone Soup

With every item added to the list, I grew a bit wearier about how I could begin delivering them. I knew I couldn't ask for it all at the same time, but I had to start somewhere. I needed to pick something significant enough to get started. Then the idea of the story of stone soup came to mind. It was an old tale about an old, penniless beggar woman who went through multiple villages asking for food, getting turned away each time, until she got a genius idea. She picked up a discarded pot and found a stone to put in it and went knocking on a door, claiming she was making "stone soup" but just needed water to get started. Met with confusion, the first person reluctantly provided her with the water after she stated she couldn't reveal the recipe but promised to come back and share a cup of it once it was made. Armed with a pot, a stone, and water, going on to the next home was easier, asking for an onion, which she was granted after the confused person saw the pot with the stone water already in place but banking on there being a plan. Each of the next homes got easier to convince as more ingredients presented themselves—carrots, celery, then chicken pieces ... the more people could see something was brewing, the more comfortable they were with donating something small to the pot. When she got to the end of the row of homes, she had acquired everything she needed, including the herbs and spices to give the soup the right flavor. She started a little fire, removed the stone, and allowed the soup to cook. When it was ready, in good faith, she returned to each home to offer the promised cup of stone soup, keeping her word, and sharing the goodness. It was never about the stone—the stone had only served as inspiration. It held mystery and the power to unlock belief. That was also my task, to get things started and get a good brew of improvement going.

So, what did I pick as my first resource to get them? Access to a remote-control tool. My instinct was that the team could hear what their end users complained about, but they couldn't see it, and without the ability to see clearly, they couldn't troubleshoot, nor describe what was needed for additional support from the other levels of IT. In addition to credibility being really low at the time, their customers didn't want to waste time talking or describing the issue for long, so a remote session solved much of that pain point. The result of getting that tool was tangible; team members felt elated to be able to do more than listen and transcribe a problem, they were finally able to take control and fix something. And measuring their resolution rates, we started to see the slight-but-steady increase in their traction with fixes. It caused a noticeable shift in their confidence with their demeanor improving with each solution they delivered remotely.

In a few months, customers began noticing that the "helpless desk" wasn't as helpless as they'd thought and that they could actually do more than just get a password reset by them. When they felt they could be of service in more ways, the end users began giving them more of their time to try to resolve issues they called them for. It was interesting to watch this unfold. With each weekly meeting, the fifteen- to twenty-minute check-in with the team, witnessed more of them bubbling over with excitement as they finally felt useful and were beginning to get positive reviews from their customers, along with the sincere thank yous.

I have to say, it was not easy knocking on that first door, my director's, to ask for access to the tool, but it was necessary, and it changed the course of that team. That first tool served as the stone to anchor the team, give them eyes and ears beyond their expectations. But then behind it came advanced privileges to active directory, then to applications, then more training. You see, as the team grew deeper in knowledge and their attitude changed to more of a "yes, we can do that" attitude, other teams took notice. They recognized the change and started cheering them on. They wanted to contribute to the tools and to helping the team advance in its knowledge. It became a Jerry McGuire thing—"Help me help you"—with them realizing that the more the help desk could do, the more work they could give to them, freeing themselves up to do other more advanced work that they desperately wanted to do but couldn't due to time constraints.

From this time in my career, the early management time,  I learned that managers try to do things the right way, but leaders, they're different. They're the ones who have to do what's right, and with that comes discomfort. Asking for things, rallying for the troops, facing negative sentiment, and a ton of conflict, that's all part of leadership. You still need to get the basics of the routine right, getting the process, the procedures, and the policies all in place to keep things moving, but to really make a difference, you start with the people. You have to know them well, know what their strengths are, what their motivators are, and be consistent in how you deal with them, with kindness and respect. And most of all, you have to be willing to give a lot of your time and energy. Without that, it doesn't matter what tools you have or what you're measuring, it will be like walking up a down escalator because the people part is the most important part of that equation.

PART 2

People First: Becoming the Leader Others Choose to Follow

CHAPTER 4

Getting to What Matters—People

The Power of People over Process

Soon after I started to get deep into my first role as manager, I realized two things. One, you can learn all you need to learn about the processes and the tools from different sources, including books and classes. And two, no one was going to give you a complete playbook on how to manage the team you were asked to manage. No one.

It was a hard reality to accept item number two, as I'd falsely assumed I'd somehow get trained to be a manager (for what reason, I have no idea … perhaps simple naivety?). I don't know, I guess deep down I couldn't grasp that you could be hired for a role for which you didn't truly already have experience, as that would be a risk to the organization, and specifically for that manager or leader who hired you.

This is where I got to understand something huge about people. We are all teachable. We're all sponges, of different types and depths. We all have the ability to look, listen, and learn, to great differing extents. What differentiates us is the *desire* to learn and how we sink ourselves into that learning. When I think of the real reason I ended up thriving as a new manager, it was because I wanted to make my manager proud of his decision to hire me. "Mr. R," I'll call him.

Mr. R was by no means perfect. He had a very strange way of onboarding me. (Perhaps that will be something I share later in this book—the do's and don'ts of onboarding.) He had a strange way of giving direction; he didn't tell you the answer to any of the questions you asked, but asked you a lot of extra questions, and then spent a good amount of time telling stories and *explaining* things that he could tell you didn't understand. His unique gift was patience and empathy. I don't believe I'd ever met anyone with the massive amount of both of these qualities, which made him both approachable and a true leader. I had many *mini lessons* from Mr. R. He was purposeful with spending time to give feedback on the metrics I shared, celebrate moments when we reached milestones, and seemingly always positive about the progress, however slow, we were making. "Upwards and onwards" and "slow and steady wins the race" were his words of encouragement. And to be frank, that released a huge pressure valve for me … I was the one putting the pressure on to move and with urgency, and perhaps it was in response to the big gap I'd seen from other departments, and from the most important part, the people we served, who yearned for better each day.

While spending time with my team lead in that first manager role, I learned that if you spend enough time with people, you'll get to know them quite well. Their armor starts to dissolve, and they become great advocates for change, especially when they feed into that formula you're putting together. I also discovered that while a person may have inherent leadership skills, they naturally know how to influence others and have followers behind and with them, that doesn't mean they want to be given management responsibilities. My team lead had such a charming, positive demeanor and was naturally patient with people. Until he wasn't. I discovered his hot buttons one day when I pushed him a bit further than he'd wanted to be pushed. Boy, was that an explosive moment. I remember feeling pinned to the wall, completely unprepared for the raised voice and the harsh tone…with the words being the least of the problems. I quickly realized that not everyone has the same ambitions; some want money, others want benefits, while others want to climb the career ladder and become leaders at different levels. And some just want the slow and steady job; they want to go to work, put in a hard day's effort, ruffle no feathers, and then collect a paycheck. They neither ask for a raise nor question company policy or mission. They just glide. And we need these gliders; in fact, they're core to every team. My team lead was definitely a glider. He was well-liked by his peers, and I liked and believed in him. Management, on the other hand, had a completely different opinion. They saw him as a *slacker, someone* who may be a bit of a shop steward, with the potential to negatively influence the team. That was enlightening.

With time and with the energy placed into the relationship, I began what my boss would later call "rewiring" of my team lead. I didn't particularly like that term, but over the years I embraced it as not necessarily something that was bad. We all come with mostly the same wires, but sometimes, somehow, the wires may get crossed. For some, it may be due to negative experiences with management. For others, it may be the pool they're in for too long with no growth or exposure to different things. And for others, it may just be childhood trauma. I learned really early on that while my role as manager required me to listen and to be empathetic, in no way was my role to be a therapist to anyone. And this was hard, as sometimes the person you're listening to shares deep truths and secrets that you're ill-equipped to handle, and responding in any particular way may cause more harm than good. Boy, do I know about that. Plenty of missteps along the way, the roles, and the people. But you learn from these moments, how to hold space for the person, to be there, to acknowledge how hard it must've been, without unpacking too deeply or trying to solve their problems. And so, with my team lead, I grew to understand that he was perfectly comfortable with being my right hand, a team lead even, but he was adamant about staying away from further management responsibilities. And that was fine. After all, wasn't I the one who a few years ago had chosen the right side of the road, being an SME, versus the left side of the road to management? Of course I was. So, I shouldn't be surprised someone else would be as well. Except, I was, and unfortunately, I was inwardly disappointed that I couldn't dislodge my team lead from whatever limiting beliefs he had and get him to realize how wonderful an assistant manager or manager he could be one day. I also had to be fine with my inability to rewire him further along that path.

Another big thing I learned really early from that role and that served me really well in future roles in leadership is that your most valuable resource in an organization is *your people.* The group of individuals you're entrusted to manage needs to be operating from their positions of greatest strength. That means a few things: one, they need to be skilled enough to do the basic work of the position; two, passionate enough to do it with excitement; and three, willing to learn along the way. The second point about passion makes a big difference, as that is what sets the table for them to get quality over quantity and to also differentiate themselves by learning at a more steady versus rapid pace. And that takes me to an important point: When you first get there as a new manager, your first job is to get to know the people, very deeply. That entails identifying their strengths and knowing what areas they have to work on (that are required for the role, not in life in general). When you get to know their strengths, that opens the door for you to place them into opportunities where they can showcase those strengths in a constructive way. It helps them shine too. "Catch them doing something good." When you start to hire people with different strengths, you start to recognize the power of the entire *team.* That they complement each other in different ways; where one person has a weakness, another has it as a strength, and they begin learning from each other. Over time, your people with weaknesses may improve in those areas, and overall, the strengths demonstrated in all the unique areas are what carry the team over big hurdles,

as the momentum grows with successes. And this is precisely the lesson; **we, as managers and leaders, set the stage for our team to show up as heroes. This is where we create the opportunity for *hero moments.***

Creating Hero Moments

We all come equipped with unique talents and strengths, that's true, but we don't naturally think of ourselves as heroes, do we? Probably not. Yet I'll challenge that we're not just heroes, we're superheroes at times. But what makes superheroes super is not necessarily their inherent skill or superpower; it's the *consistency* with which they show up and how they use their gifts for *good.*

Again, common people are heroes every day, though they don't always know it. The question is, who is seeing them as such? My hope is that there is always someone who stops to witness the magic of their superpowers, what they do in silence and in service of others. And therein lies our responsibility as managers.

When I crossed over from being a sole contributor, that SME I'd thought I was destined to be, I hadn't realized that being a manager, and eventually a leader, was more about other people than about me. I truly believe when you're a leader, your core responsibility is to provide people with the opportunity to succeed and to reach their maximum potential, guiding and supporting them along the way. You have to see into who they are deep down, not just what they show you on the surface. I know that sounds a bit invasive, but it truly isn't.

To get the real value out of individuals, you do have to set them on the path to success by capitalizing on their true potential, their *areas of strength,* and their *desire to work within it.* Your people are your first customers, and thinking of how they experience you as their manager/leader, and how they experience the workday, is huge in how they fulfill their role and step into their strength. You, as a manager and a true leader, need to get to the root of what makes them tick and give them an opportunity to display it.

While I was in my first role as manager, I was given the opportunity to take on more responsibilities, acquiring network operations center tasks, and then later, after a merger with another company, taking on a much broader oversight of different support departments. Was I ready each time for that promotion and added set of responsibilities? Probably not. But Mr. R knew that I had demonstrated not just potential, I had delivered. He promoted me not once, but twice, partially on potential, but also having witnessed what I had demonstrated by way of passion, patience, and a perpetually positive can-do attitude that inspired the same in the people I led. Mr. R placed me on the hero stage and allowed me to have the hero moments that I did for many years to follow.

Fast-forward to how this manifested in hero moments for others. I recall the moment I convinced Mr. R that despite having a limited budget to hire, that to address the capacity problem we faced with the mounting needs of the department, we could explore hiring interns for the summer and assigning them a single, core project to complete over that short period, a win-win. We get the resource needed for a short duration on a key project, and that person gets experience and a little money to help them out with their personal expenses. In walks my first intern, dressed complete with jeans, T-shirt, cowboy boots, and leather belt. (I don't think he had the matching hat, though my memory is a bit fuzzy now.) I could've dismissed him right there for failing to attempt to present in a predictable outfit for an interview (even as an intern). Instead, I was intrigued by his personality and the brazenness with which he carried himself. I learned that he had some deep talent in coding, something we couldn't quite afford to hire for at the time and something we needed in order to enhance our self-service portal. Hiring this intern turned out to be the best temporary decision we made that summer; he blended in perfectly, despite how different he was. Given the chance to demonstrate his skill, he showed up in spades. At the end of the summer, I knew I couldn't keep him on the team, but I hated losing him, despite knowing full well he had to continue his education. Years later, he confided that nothing moved him more in his career than that internship, and that he had carried the motivation and energy from working with my team into a technical management role he loved and was proud of.

Over time, I grew to understand that all teams crave recognition, and that giving them not just individual attention, but a larger stage to shine on, was absolutely necessary. This is where finding a forum for recognition goes a long way. While at that management role that later turned into a director role, I found a community of similar subject matter experts in the Help Desk Institute, which held monthly meetings for thought leadership exchange and also hosted an annual "Analyst of the Year" competition to identify the talent with the best overall customer service skills. I nominated one of our very best analysts one year, and with it came the vetting process by judges, but more importantly, the opportunity to be recognized with all finalists in front of management from the different companies in the New York region. What I didn't fully expect was that my nominee would win! They were elated to be called up as the winner that evening, receiving a glass trophy with their name engraved on it and a gift card. It wasn't enough to simply enjoy that day, I wanted to blast his win from the tallest of buildings. And to be fair, it did go to his head a bit; the analyst not only felt like a winner, a hero, he acted like it. He began demonstrating his skills in a more constructive way, helping other colleagues achieve stronger technical skills, gaining competency for the whole team over time. Once again, a win-win.

From that point on, every year, I challenged my managers of different teams to identify talent delivering exceptional service, nominate them for awards, submit them for recognition opportunities, and do the hard work of elevating recognition (the limelight) to others.

Another example was with this bright, jovial service desk analyst we'd hired initially as a consultant and then quickly converted to full-time. She was Doris Day incarnate, complete with blond hair and bright blue eyes. She spoke with confidence, had strong listening skills, and most of all, was a go-getter. I'll call her Doris for the remainder of this story. I loved having her on the team and felt she energized those around her. Doris was one of the last individuals I recommended we nominate for the Analyst of the Year spot, for all those reasons. It was no surprise that she won locally and then quickly went on to win regionally. That set her up to go to the finals, the "nationals" where she would compete for the worldwide award.

That year, I had recognized that it was time to move on to the next stop in my career, taking on a new role within a new organization, and my resignation fell around the time that the national HDI conference was being held. I would naturally have wanted to attend the conference, but having given my notice, with only a few days to wrap up my transition activities, it was hard to see how I could pull this off. You see, it's not just nominating and cheering someone as they go for the gold that is necessary; it's your presence that matters most.

Doing What's Right and Not Just What's Easy

Let me finish that story. When I gave my notice, on my birthday, my entire team appeared to be devastated. A lot of people had gotten promoted and were growing there, and they wanted everything to stay the same, but I also needed to do what was right for myself. It was time to move on.

Then came the decision that I had to make, while I wiped away tears and ate birthday cake with the team—should I stay or should I go? Doris was not shy about telling me how she had been *emulating* me, following my lead, always looking to me for guidance and encouragement. I felt the pressure to support her and the awkwardness of the timing of it all. I found clear and complete support from Mr. R, urging me to go to the conference and be there for Doris.

And so to the conference I went. Doris was thrilled to have the support she did, and I was thrilled to be able to witness her excitement and feel the anticipation of that announcement. I gave her a thumbs up on her black suit and watched as she squirmed in her brand-new, black patent-leather heels. She was in the kind of pain that makes it hard to keep a smile on and presents the potential of a trip and fall while walking up stairs and onto a stage. But I knew I had one more thing to offer—my shoes. I looked down at hers and it appeared we were the same size. So, I offered my black leather pumps to swap with hers. Swapping the shoes, she felt immediate relief wearing mine, broken in from continuous wear but in otherwise excellent shape. I was going to sit in brand-new black Coach pumps, while she got to breathe in mine.

Then they called her name as the winner! She got up and gracefully walked onto the stage, effortlessly gliding to the podium, grinning ear to ear. She wasn't simply smiling; she was beaming as she looked out to the audience of two thousand-plus members. I don't know if the spotlight had shone on me that moment instead of her that I would've been any happier or prouder. This moment was pure gold, for her, but more importantly, for me. I watched her accept the glass trophy, listened to her express her gratitude, thanking those who had impacted her career, and I felt completely at peace with everything. I loved that the hero of the day was on the stage and had the limelight.

Good Intentions, *hit Execution

Then there were those moments when you saw what could've been a hero moment turn into a total zero moment. I called this *good intentions, *hit execution*. I do inherently believe that people are generally good, and their intentions are also generally good. Somewhere along the line, they falter on their execution. They missed the mark, and the screw-up was audible, visible, and more importantly, memorable. But you know what, no one is perfect. We all make mistakes, and we all have the ability to rectify them. Mistakes, as I say, refine you, they don't define you … unless you let them. When you keep ignoring your own mistakes or repeatedly making the same ones, that's when it hurts you and others.

There was a consultant that we had hired and converted for our service desk, a brilliant technical talent with a very smooth style of communication. He had the ability to smooth-talk just about anyone while on the phone, following his technical support instructions, getting them to climb off a ledge to safety. He had observed how we rewarded talent, recognizing individuals (consultants) and converting the best, handing out bonuses, nominating individuals for awards, promoting and compensating them. No doubt, this was a gold mine. We thought we had him in the gold pile. He was also aware that he was working at a service desk and that despite the consistent track record of individuals getting promoted into other roles from there, they still had to do the work and abide by the rules. And that's where things got a bit murky. I'll call this one a Bozo moment. Our analyst, who thought he was brilliant (let's call him that), also knew that all of our calls were not just monitored but also recorded. Not only was it our practice to occasionally listen in on random calls to get a pulse for how analysts were doing, but we could also pull a recording at any moment. That's when we discovered our brilliant one's missteps with clients; he was engaging in sex talk while on the phone giving troubleshooting steps. He wasn't on the light side either. It was heavy-handed, complete with deep breathing, clearly inappropriate language, and promises that should've never been made in that context. It wasn't just once, twice, or a couple more times; it was constant and with several customers who apparently enjoyed the experience and never raised a complaint. Again, just because you can, doesn't mean you should. His error in judgment was huge, our decision to terminate was quick. He may have had good intentions to provide technical services (among other services, who knows?), but his execution was clearly *hit.

The last example I'll give is one that came later in my leadership journey. It was my hire of a director, someone I saw as a superb talent, full of vivaciousness, common sense, and a deep desire to perform. Lady X, we'll call her. She was a mature woman, in the upper half of her career, with significant experience under her belt.

While Lady X was a go-getter, someone who knew how to execute, I realized with time that she was most comfortable with the inner circle of the team I had (her colleagues) and that she played up to the attention of leaders above her. As I added positions under her, I began noticing a strange dynamic with her direct reports. They were quiet in her presence, but in meetings or settings when she wasn't around, very vocal and happy. But with her around, the opposite—very reserved, almost guarded. The years went on, with the team under her expanding in count and responsibility, doing good work, but in the annual anonymous employee feedback survey, they used strong language to share their dissent and their disdain with her style. It turns out Lady X cracked a strong whip behind closed doors. I also learned that she spoke poorly of my leadership style behind my back to her staff and to her peers. She assumed that sweet-talking management would do the trick and having a high level of energy was sufficient. It wasn't.

Before long, the team she led was becoming very demoralized, with evidence in increased absenteeism and the rise of complaints to HR leaders on individual infractions. They recommended we hold a focus group discussion for the team, with HR, so they can uncover the problem. I later heard tales of continuous browbeating and humiliation of the staff. We even started to get complaints from other departments about how abusive Lady X became toward their staffs. It was becoming clear that despite the overall technical performance of this leader being quite positive, the toxic traits she displayed were detrimental to the health and well-being of the team, and to be fair, the entire IT department. More importantly, they didn't represent my leadership style and tolerating them any further was also a reflection on me as a leader. While I wanted to give her as long a time to remediate her style and improve her execution, I knew that tolerating the bad behavior was pulling us further into an abyss of negativity. We were on the cusp of losing the positive spirit that our department was known for. Executing that termination, for cause, was by far one of the most difficult things I've had to do as a leader. I hated having to do that, despite its necessity. In the end, I learned a very strong lesson. **We, as leaders, are not responsible for the delivery of every person on the team, nor their style; we're responsible for *giving them the opportunity to deliver,* supporting them through it, and for cheering them along the way. In addition, not all potential is ready and not all leaders are equipped to be therapists, nor should they be.**

You can do your part with compassion and still not reach them. Sometimes the most humane thing is to let go, even if it hurts.

The experience with Lady X taught me that not everyone can be saved through work alone. Some wounds show up as defiance, as disruption, as exhaustion. I wasn't equipped for what she was carrying. But I was always in her corner, and I always hoped she would find peace, wherever she went from there.

CHAPTER 5

Discovering the Platinum Rule

Learning Human Psychology

I didn't mention this earlier, but I was actually not an IT major in college—in fact, I only took one management information systems class as part of the business management major I ended up going for. And within that were two very critical classes— Accounting 101 and Psychology 101. While I want to say they're a close tie in the importance to me, I know that would be stretching the truth. The reality is that I learned more from that single class in psychology than just about any other course I took in college. People fascinated me. The way they think, the way they communicate, with all their voices, their eyes, hands, and…. their silence. There's nothing more complex than the human psyche (in my humble opinion).

This is why I thought the study of body language, way back then, was so interesting. Many of the early lessons I learned stayed with me in my career and personal life. But to know how to read people and body language and have strong intuition about them, well, that's a major edge. We live on this planet with over eight billion other humans. We've had a common language all of these centuries until now—it's the human mind and the human emotion. We all have these, regardless of where and when we grew up, and how we live. Though we're all very similar, I have to acknowledge that we're completely different, each and every one of us—so much so that we have unique DNA that's impossible to replicate. Unique fingerprints, voiceprints too. Even identical twins aren't exactly identical. That's the exact reason I was always puzzled by the Golden Rule, which directed people to treat others as they'd want to be treated. But why? Are we to assume that everyone is the same? Or that we all like the same things? Do we all want and need exactly the same thing? I know this may feel like I'm getting philosophical here … but bear with me for a moment.

Since we all have unique DNA, and we all have completely unique life experiences, I'd say that even within a single family, siblings have different experiences by virtue of their chronological order and what was happening when in their family's life. So, in essence, it's impossible to assume that everyone wants and needs the same thing. True, we may all want and need the basics like safety, food, shelter, and love. But aside from these critical items, everything else is a wild card. So, I couldn't really wrap my head around the Golden Rule, ever. It just didn't work for me.

This rule also got challenged when I started to realize that it was counterproductive to try to manage a team and apply a one-size-fits-all approach. It's the same insane idea as punishing all for the sins of the few—why would we do that? Simply put, because it's easier, not better. So, with little time in management, I realized that I had to customize my way for members on the team, not because I necessarily wanted to (initially), but because I had to. Some team members liked it when I stopped by and said good morning, asking how they were doing, while others really wanted to be heads down doing their work, happy to get a wave as I walked by. There were those who seemed to need more reassurance, while others asked a lot of questions about instructions, and yet others who had little to no curiosity about the processes and procedures laid out. Everyone was different. Everyone came with their own blueprint. I learned this the hard way too, when I tried to cookie-cutter performance reviews the first year I had to conduct them, thinking everyone gets a half-hour, reads the review, and signs off while in front of me.

Boy, was that off. For the same reasons I mentioned before, assuming that what works for one will work for all is a major misconception. For one, some people have language barriers, and they may not understand common expressions or basic vocabulary, so they may need things explained differently. Others may have a need for privacy and to take time to digest the message alone, not under scrutiny. While others still may want to get into more of a debate, challenging every point and asking for evidence. **The point is not that you have to customize in advance for each person; it's that you have to recognize what each person needs by way of treatment and be willing to give it to them.**

Watching and Learning the Different Styles

For a while, I was observing different leaders as they demonstrated their styles in handling people—their staffs, colleagues, bosses. They too all seemed to be different. No two leaders were exactly the same. It confused me for a bit, as I couldn't quite find the North Star for how to treat people, up, down, and sideways. Until I attended a conference, and though I can't recall which keynote speaker actually shared the concept of the "Platinum Rule," I can confidently say that my entire universe completely shifted the moment I made contact with it. And it hasn't reverted ever since!

The Platinum Rule says to treat people as *they* want to be treated. Vastly different than how *you'd* want to be treated. The Platinum Rule recognizes our differences and that there is no one-size-fits-all. Trying to treat everyone exactly the same then becomes a recipe for disaster. Of course, you want to be fair to all and provide nurture and support to all, but taking a completely socialist stance and eradicating differences also then devalues our diversity. And it is our diversity as humans that actually brings out our strengths. Think of it this way—if you were the math brainiac in your class and grew up loving numbers, then becoming the analytical genius in your community, would it be fair to force you to take on a role in the artistic world of marketing or design? It wouldn't be playing to your strengths. Even if there was a need for the manpower, it would put you at a disadvantage, eliminating your key strength and focusing on your weakness. A million more examples can be made around how diverse our strengths (and weaknesses) are.

The Grand Awareness Moment

Coming back from that conference, sitting on a plane, that's when the lightbulb went on. I can almost recall the feeling I had when I grasped this key concept fully. To be truly successful with people, you had to watch, listen, and feel with your heart and your mind—learn about a person, well before you can work with them, and definitely before you can even begin to lead them. And in the first few years I mingled with others in management, I saw time and time again how many who failed to gain strong followership from their teams, their staff, also seemed to fail to apply the Platinum Rule. They were stuck following the Golden Rule, falling back on their own experiences, going back to what they had wanted, needed, and assumed would work for all! Big mistake … huge. And it often cost them greatly.

Remember that time when I shared my assumption about my team lead, who had been with the company for upward of a decade, was trying to naturally step into the manager role? Why wouldn't he? More prestige, more money, the chance to help others on the team—mentoring, training. It didn't make sense at first why he would adamantly refuse to take what I initially thought would be the natural next step. Until I got to know him better. He wanted none of the things I wanted. He was more than satisfied with his progression. His definition of success was far simpler, and he was fully satisfied with continuing to live in a two-bedroom apartment in his neighborhood and eventually collecting the pension he would receive. That was his happiness formula. Clearly, it was very different from my own, but perhaps there are more people who share elements of that formula.

Another example I stumbled upon was with my first administrative assistant. She was there only a year before I started. I could see how smart and vibrant she was, despite her constant mentioning of how old and close to retirement she was. It didn't add up to me—how could someone so bright want to be an admin? How could that be fulfilling for her? Except I didn't fully know her story back then, and when I did, it quickly made sense. Some people, while they appear very professional and outwardly chipper, have suffered a significant amount in their lives, carrying the weight of a family, the burden of care for a handicapped child or spouse, or suffering from ailments that aren't visible to others. They may want what's tangible and no additional challenges. Not because they aren't up to learning, but because their souls are wary—they're simply exhausted. They want to be great at what they do but don't need to be overly visible.

But then there are those who are firecrackers, from the day they walked in with their cowboy boots on. You have to pay attention to the colorful streaks of hair, the way they tackle a stretch assignment, or volunteer for work that others wouldn't want. They yearn to be challenged. They are the ones who step up intentionally, wanting more. The "more" sometimes isn't just responsibility or compensation—sometimes it's more time.

I gradually learned that to apply the Platinum Rule, you have to become like a rubber band, stretching and bending in different ways and for different reasons. The only thing is you have to be careful you don't stretch yourself beyond your physical (and mental) limits for fear of snapping. It's true, while applying the Golden Rule sounds like a good idea, the most honorable thing is to be constantly applying the Platinum Rule. But, beware, this is at times more draining than you think. I had a direct report who would regularly knock on my office door, asking if I had a minute. Usually, this was around 4:55 p.m. on a workday. And his minute was generally fifty-eight minutes long. By then, I'd missed not one, but two trains on the LIRR and was definitely off my schedule for prepping dinner for the kiddos. Another colleague liked to bounce ideas off me, but her way of doing this was different. She asked a lot of questions, without telling me what the problem was, and when she felt I was giving her deep attention, she'd spring the problem on me. It wasn't always easy keeping the frustration levels down, but I knew that it was just her style.

What was more obvious over time is that by spending the time to get to know people, to learn who they are deep inside, paying attention to their wants and needs, it built a bond between us. It also laid the foundation for building trust. When people see that you are truly interested in them as humans and you're willing to spend time and energy with them, they let you see who they are. They also begin to feel a connection with you, one that is far more powerful than any command-and-control approach would bring. In fact, the latter only creates distance and not true allegiance.

From Manager to Leader: The Shift That Changed Everything

For the decades that followed, I made sure that the Platinum Rule was what I preached when coaching and mentoring staff that reported to me and colleagues or staff on other teams. I wanted to make sure as many people as I knew who wanted to make a difference learned that this Platinum Rule was truly at the root of our humanity. To ignore or make light of it would be ignoring a mountain that would perpetually get in your way in life, whether for your career or your personal endeavors. I wrote about the Platinum Rule in articles, I used it in my coaching sessions, and I applied it regularly in my personal life, even with my two children. Until this day, I think the biggest shift I experienced in my style, transforming from a manager to a leader, came the day I recognized and embraced the Platinum Rule. And for that I'm truly grateful.

CHAPTER 6

The Essence of Leadership

Leadership in the Raw

Until I started my first role as a manager, I can honestly say that I didn't understand what leadership is. I, like many people, associated it with a title. You're the boss, you're the leader. In simple terms, it's someone who is in charge of people, gives them orders, and makes the big bucks. Well, not so much.

It turns out that most of that is peripheral to what leadership really is. The best definition I ever stumbled upon was from John C. Maxwell: "Leadership is influence, nothing more, nothing less." Maxwell, one of the world's foremost leadership thinkers and authors, has spent decades teaching that leadership isn't about authority or position; it's about the ability to inspire and impact others. That simple. One word. Influence. The ability to influence someone makes you a leader. Well, if we break it down, to be a leader, you have to have followers. To have followers, you have to get people to do or think in a certain way. And to do that, they have to be convinced that they should, otherwise they're just pretending. So, it turns out he's 100 percent right—what true leaders do is influence people, not force them to think and do certain things. And how do they do that exactly? That's the key.

There are many books on leadership, the formula for leadership, the tips and tricks of leading. Methodologies, master classes, mentorships—you name it, it exists. One of my favorite simplified explanations of the difference between leadership and management is this one by Warren Bennis, a pioneer in leadership studies: "Managers do things right, and leaders do the right thing." That's gold right there. You see, managers are commissioned to enact a course that's already been defined, and to hold their teams accountable for delivering a service or product. Managers manage people through instruction, reviewing progress, and correcting the course when necessary. Leaders, on the other hand, design the course, solicit ideas, and motivate the team to deliver with distinction.

Going back to the purest definition of what leadership is, influence, that means that in essence, anyone can lead if they can get others to share a vision and then follow them in executing it. That's why many people who are sole contributors in their companies are seen as leaders; they have the ability to convince others with their thoughts, their words, and at times, just their actions. Nowadays, there's even a newly minted role called "influencer," and it refers to people on social media who have amassed a following by sharing their thoughts, demonstrating activities, or reviewing products and creating a movement around these. These *influencers* live on many platforms like TikTok, Instagram, YouTube, and even Amazon, making it a significant revenue channel.

I'm spending some time with the concept of leadership now because it is foundational to transforming an organization; in fact, it is foundational to culture. And the best definition of culture that I've come across in all my years in the business world is this: "Culture is the behavior that senior leadership either *displays* or *tolerates*." Take note of these words—display and tolerate. That means to shape culture, *the way we do things around here*, you have to model a certain style of behavior, and you have to react to behaviors around you. The word *tolerate* isn't accidental here; it has a negative connotation, so saying that a leader tolerates a behavior (that is negative) means he or she is giving the green light for it to continue, and so it festers. I would also argue that rewarding positive attributes and behaviors also models what good and great look like, and that's another way of displaying what the ideal is. Now, let's dig a little deeper into leadership qualities, so we know the key ingredients that shape leadership.

The ABCs of Leadership

In observing different leadership styles over multiple decades, I found a range of behaviors among them. Some were loud and boisterous, others were more subdued and collected. The way they walked and talked differed; how they analyzed a situation and took action also differed. But these were all attributed to personal *styles*. And it's all related to the *human factor*. So, our experiences, as followers, will differ depending on our own personality and theirs. That's natural. But what I did find that was unequivocally common among all those whom I deemed true leaders were three qualities: authenticity, boldness, and compassion. These are what I call the ABCs of leadership; without them, you struggle to gain followership and keep it. Let's unpack this further.

Authenticity

Authenticity is about being truly you. It's being the only version of you, wherever you go. This means letting people see who you really are and sharing truths and more of yourself. It is about allowing yourself to be vulnerable, sharing what really concerns you, while knowing where the boundaries are. It doesn't mean you have to cry publicly, but if it happens at a very sensitive moment, it is seen as being human. It also means being consistent with your thoughts and words on your beliefs and living them. It is *walking the talk*.

Boldness

So many people have dreams of what they want to do and be, yet they don't find it easy to get there. Oftentimes, they fail to take that next step of *execution,* which makes all the difference. It takes a ton of courage to do what scares you, stepping out of your comfort zone into the unknown … taking risks, facing the possibility of failure. I talked about this earlier when I shared many of my own fears and how I viewed the world—and finding the courage to act was hard but necessary. Leaders dare to be brave and to do what scares them. They follow through on their promises to others and also to themselves. This means being consistent, even when feeling unsure. Boldness is about doing the thing that is outside of your normal warm and fuzzy zone, even when you're not feeling ready, because it's "doing what's right and not just what's easy" (this one is a favorite self-quote, which I live and die by). Leaders just go ahead, challenging the status quo, stepping on some toes, asking for forgiveness and not permission *sometimes*. They aren't shackled by fear of failure, and they share the belief that "mistakes refine you, they don't define you" (another favorite self-quote).

Compassion

Last time I checked, we are all human first and then a myriad of other roles in this world. We must always be in touch with the fact that we have a thousand more things in common than in difference. Always remembering to lead with heart and caring about those around you is what sets you apart as a leader. *Empathy* is the key to influencing hearts and minds. This quote by Theodore Roosevelt is so true: *"People don't care how much you know until they know how much you care."* At the root of being human is the desire to be loved and cared for. Compassion is by far the greatest gift you can give others, whether you lead them or follow them or they're simply in one of your life's circles. Compassion isn't saved just for people you like; it's even for people you dislike. You never really know what people's lives and journeys have been, so being compassionate shows up as giving people the benefit of the doubt, assuming positive intent, and trying to see the good in them instead of the not-so-good.

It used to be that a leader was seen as this distant figure, who kept their personal lives closed and remote from their team and colleagues, spoke with strong and certain terms, and didn't make time to be with the people. That was the *command-and-control type of* leader, who used power to get movement. But that's like carrying a rock uphill; it's heavy and exhausting. Isn't letting a rock roll downhill much easier and faster? Of course it is. That's what influence is, and it starts with showing who you are, taking firm and consistent action, and caring about people in a way that matters.

I'll go back to an early memory of my time working for Mr. R. We were situated downtown in NYC, and the majority of the staff had to commute via railroad and subway. The occasional leader, like Mr. R., drove in. Despite a two-hour commute, he would walk into the office and casually stop in to say good morning to everyone, lingering to chat about how the weekend went, and any celebrated occasion he'd heard about. He shared his own stories often, letting the team hear about how his daughter was doing and some odd mishaps with the plumbing in the house. What he did wasn't hard, but it was purposeful. He carved out time to look, listen, and learn about his people, and to share stories. That morning walk, and the consistent way he traipsed around the office in pursuit of an afternoon snack or cup of coffee, chatting with members of the team, it went a long way. It built trust and allowed him to influence the team. He was more than just nice; he was *present,* and that was the biggest present of all. To add to his style of engagement was his ability to take definite action when necessary. It was certain that if we went to him with a problem, he would hear us out, ask for options for execution, and challenge us for alternatives that were bolder but more effective. While he was diplomatic, he was known to be assertive and not one to shy away from taking unpopular action, upsetting the apple cart. He did what's right, which, for sure, wasn't always easy. And with that consistency in how he showed up, it built a sense of psychological safety; we knew he had our back, so we had his.

Mr. R. was one of a few leaders who exemplified the word leader. He led from the heart but always checked himself from the head. He had, from what I could see, the mindset of a gardener, and intuitively applied the Platinum Rule, treating people as they wanted to be treated.

How Leaders Are Gardeners

A few years ago, I attended a conference and listened to the wise words of Stephen M.R. Covey speaking about leaders of people needing to have the mindset of a gardener—creating conditions for them to flourish and blossom. This is very true. Leaders need to cultivate the conditions that allow growth in each individual similarly to how a gardener cultivates the ideal setting for each plant to grow; different locations, soil type, time to plant, time to fertilize, and even time to sow. But isn't that giving them what they want and need, similarly to the Platinum Rule? Absolutely it is. I personally found this analogy to be remarkable because I often find myself lost for hours in my own garden, tending to each area differently and thinking about the same thing. It never ceases to amaze me how some plants need maximum sun, others need shade, some need constant moisture, others barely need watering, some need regular fertilizing, others once a season, etc. The more I learn about gardening, the more I realize I need to continue to learn, and that's the mindset of leaders too.

One of the stories Covey told during this discussion was especially impactful. He spoke about Death Valley, a desert valley in Eastern California in the northern Mojave Desert, as being the hottest place on earth, with temperatures reaching over 130 degrees Fahrenheit, and nothing growing there for those reasons. He mentioned that one year (I don't recall if it was 2001 or 2005), it rained six inches there, something that never happens. And miraculously, vegetation started to appear everywhere, from a single downpour! He reasoned that there were seeds under that flat, hard soil that would only germinate under the right conditions, even waiting decades to do so. And what they witnessed was a surfacing of a green spread that they'd never seen before.

Taking this back to the gardening analogy, people are very much like plants. They need all the right conditions to flourish. We can even think about those who love the outdoors and others who prefer being indoors. Some plants need direct sunlight, others prefer the shade. Some need moist soil, others prefer dry soil. Some will need a little boost each season, with some peat moss or fertilizer, while others don't need much to start sprouting. And let's not forget the many varieties of plants, the bulbs, the annuals, the perennials, the succulents, the shrubs, the trees … you get the picture. There are countless types of plants, and each variety needs its unique conditions. Much like people.

Getting back to thinking about leadership's mission, it's all about understanding what each person needs. Do they need constant direction or do they prefer complete autonomy? Do they need continuous feedback and praise or do they prefer occasional and minimal acknowledgment and in a more formalized way? Are they interested in stretching their skillset and taking on vast new challenges or do they prefer very routine, known work patterns? And what specifically are their strengths, so they can be placed in their space of maximum strengths? It all makes sense when you really think about it. The role of a leader is a nurturer, a guide, a cultivator of talent. But if he/she doesn't provide the appropriate conditions, it can spell disaster for the individual they're leading.

Take, for example, sudden climate changes in the workforce, situations where a merger or acquisition considerably changes the work environment, from what work is being done by whom, to the format it gets delivered, to the audience it is being delivered to, to all the rules changing overnight. Similarly to a sudden ice storm in June, after all the perennial plants have begun to bloom and are in their happy sprouting phase, the ice comes down and wilts all the plants, which can't survive in such cold climates at certain stages of growth maturity.

So here are some things to consider as a leader (with the mindset of a gardener):

1. **The role they're in.** What individual is needed in what role (what plant serves what purpose)—the appropriate skillset matching for the individual role is key. For example, you're unlikely to place a developer in a service desk role and vice versa.

2. **The resources they need.** What resources does the individual need, including work environment, training, supporting peers—similar to what soil type is needed, the amount of sun, water, and supplemental nutrients when planting.

3. **The care and feeding.** What does the individual need to mature in their role—this is guidance, feedback, coaching, and even mentoring—similar to specific fertilizers needed for specific plants, and even pruning and thinning routines at different times of the year.

4. **The redirection warranted.** What corrective actions/ improvement plan does the person need to help redirect them onto the right path; similar to when we see signs of drying leaves, infected branches, or even rotting roots on a plant—each has its own remedy.

5. **The expanded outlook.** What can be done to grow this person further and expand them into the next role—similar to evaluating the size of the pot the plant is in and when it has outgrown its current pot or needs to be transplanted into a different location with more space/better conditions for its next stage of growth. Some may even be OK with cross-pollinating or propagating other plants.

The more you take an interest in learning about the uniqueness of the people you lead, the more you're inclined to figure out what makes them tick, how to tease out their very best, and help them shine. And that's precisely what strong leaders do. But this all takes patience—*a ton of patience, in fact.* Similarly to how a gardener starts off with a flat plot, and has to knead the soil, rake it, fertilize, plant, and irrigate it, there's a ton of waiting and watching (and praying). There is no guarantee that every individual you'll lead will be an ultimate success; after all, much of this is on the  individual's desire to succeed. **Yet the *role of the leader is to continuously cultivate the optimal environment for the individual to succeed and to give them every opportunity to do so.*** When the people you lead feel that you truly care about them as individuals, and are rooting for them and their success, they give you their best, they show up and perform beyond your (and their) wildest dreams. But you, as a leader, just have to *believe in the process* and be willing to do the work, believe in the future. That's why my advice remains this: *Plant the garden.* People who plant gardens believe in the future. And when people thrive, that's where the magic happens. That's when they become the heroes they were destined to become; it was always in their seed.

I've seen firsthand how a leader's presence, good or bad, can change everything. In fact, there were many moments throughout my career when that reality hit hard. But more on these in the next chapter.

CHAPTER 7

How Leadership Shows Up

I can't emphasize enough the importance of leadership in developing people. Leaders not only influence people along their work journey, but they also light the torch and then show the path. You learn from them and with them, and those lessons stay with you beyond a role or a company; they seep into the rest of your life. I will share stories, many stories, of leadership moments that had real impact, and these will be some of the best and some of the worst of moments. In all cases, they too were moments of truth.

Hero Moments—Terrific Leadership

One of the main things I found we go to leaders for is direction, especially when matters appear to be complex. Leaders have a way of looking at the world with a unique lens, to synthesize what's important out of the complexity, and to simplify that for their teams. I remember when I led a large service management operation at an insurance company, there were constant complaints about how hiring managers couldn't get their new hires productive for weeks, with necessary tasks lingering unnecessarily. Witnessing this frustration on both sides, with the technical teams feeling overwhelmed by the barrage of escalations, made this a call to action. There had to be a way to simplify the process. I assembled my team and asked them to brainstorm around what was critical for 80 percent of the new hires to be productive on day one. They easily came up with the list, which included an assigned work location (office/cubicle), a PC or laptop, a login to the system, an email, a desk phone, and access to the main application they use in the department. Those were six or seven items that consistently got requested, and some were requirements (like the work location) to facilitate delivery. The team began *designing* a simple one-page online form, with minimal fields to complete, then built in a workflow approval step, and we launched this as the IT onboarding process. It was simple (minimal steps, no instruction necessary); it was solid (it worked every time, no failures); and it scaled (could be carried out across the entire organization). The best part of this was the collaboration with the teams, including HR, facilities, and tele-com, to ensure we captured exactly what was critical, and nothing more, and then built that into the *simple* process. The results, a big exhale of relief, on both sides. The IT team felt they had something concrete that they could use to consistently get new staff onboarded with ease; and on the hiring manager side (the customer), they felt there were known steps, timeframes, and consistency in how the work was carried out. It took a good level of collaboration to lead and execute that project. Simple takes time—you have to apply the laws of subtraction, eliminating all the noise, the clutter, the redundant steps and activities, to distill what's purely necessary. And it takes leadership to keep pushing, asking for more scrutiny, more refine-ment, more testing, more communication. Less takes more, and it more or less works in the end. When this onboarding process was delivered and embraced, the IT team felt championed because their needs were met, and the user community felt championed because their needs were also met—it was a win-win.

Another thing great leaders do is they take the time to *fix what's broken*. They don't just acknowledge a problem and ignore it; they tackle it head-on. The long-standing problems, the messy ones, the ones that waste an extra five minutes every day but add up to countless hours each year. They tackle politics, team dynamics, and culture. Earlier on, I shared the story about the "helpless desk" and how we started a weeklong tour/rotation through the business units at the hospitals to bridge the gap in business awareness as well as recharge the team's morale. This was a huge undertaking, but it was well worth the effort and had a long-term, cascading effect on the entire IT organization as well as the business. I also encountered an issue with another technology team that was poorly managed and had low productivity levels. It appeared they were *busy* on the surface, but no one, in any accurate measure, could actually tell me what they did each day. They simply didn't measure their productivity because they didn't consistently track their work. That was a big problem. It's true that you can't manage what you can't measure. Working closely with several managers at each site, we started quantifying the unique KPIs—key performance indicators that were worth capturing and we baselined them. We placed them into a balanced scorecard, incorporating every staff member on it, and measuring it monthly. Every staff member had access to their performance, their "numbers," and they could also see where they ranked. It initially got some pushback, including from the managers themselves, until they started to see the change. Suddenly, they got to understanding how to manage capacity and demand, the impact of absenteeism on this, and how to correlate customer satisfaction with resolution effectiveness and efficiency. We essentially fixed what was broken—the way we managed the work and how it was delivered. Not only did this improve the customer experience but it also increased engagement levels with team members who felt they were part of the formula and in full awareness and control of their own performance.

Beyond looking to *simplify* and *fix what's broken*, great leaders spend the most time *listening to learn*. Their listening skills make all the difference because they give them an advantage with people. When people feel heard, they become open, more cooperative, and they do better work for you. Listening for ideas on how to fix a problem or improve a process is one thing, but paying attention to body language and observing conflict, that's a totally different thing. In one of the teams I led, I had director- and senior director-level staff. They had very diverse backgrounds, unique strengths, and strong personalities. At one point, I began observing a conflict brewing between two team members. It was displayed in meetings, complaints shared with me privately, and a level of tension increasing day by day. I realized it would be sticky to get in the middle of the conflict with these two individuals but also very necessary. Organizing a meeting to have them speak openly, sharing their viewpoints and pain points, was critical, and moderating the exchange so things didn't get overly heated was challenging but worth it. In the end, it was far better to have things out in the open, hold space for them to *debate* and *negotiate* next steps in a safe zone, versus allowing hostility to grow. I realized that the longer I allowed the passive-aggressive behavior to continue, the more resentment festered and the bonds of camaraderie would weaken. There's no place for that on a strong team, and so you do what you must—you listen to learn and you help find middle ground. It never has to be a win-lose scenario; it should always be a win-win. Maybe no one person gets everything they wanted, but they get most of what they really needed. And doing this in a respectful way makes all the difference.

Great leaders provide a psychologically safe environment for teams to thrive. They listen with intent, collaborate, and channel the energy from the team into action. They provide a forum for individuals to share their thoughts and to devise action plans without fear of failing. And you know what's more? They make it fun. When team members come to work and have fun, it becomes a light and lively environment where people thrive. Problems get solved, team members who fail get helped up and encouraged to move on or try again, and when a team member succeeds, everyone celebrates. That is the type of culture you build to elevate people. And it has a positive ripple effect on your customers. The genuine, happy smiles of your employees influence the way their customers engage with them and how they perceive and experience their service.

Zero Moments—Toxic Leadership

I know the word toxic is a strong one, and it's often used with respect to describe culture. However, as we mentioned earlier, culture is *the behavior that senior leaders either display or tolerate.* And that's precisely why we find that toxic leadership creates toxic culture.

In an earlier chapter, I described my interaction with such a toxic leader—Z-man. He thrived on minimizing people, shrinking them with his negative comments, sabotaging their energy, cornering them at every opportunity to question them in unnecessary ways. Yes, he was toxic. Everyone reporting to him felt that way. But he was overtly obvious, so you could see it a mile away. Even though he wasn't a threatening figure physically (he was actually quite scrawny as I recall), his words carried weight, and you couldn't help but feel heavy and somewhat sullied once you talked to him.

Such is the effect of leaders who thrive on a desire to command and control. They consider their role as superiors an *entitlement,* not a responsibility. Z-man was a classic case of narcissism. He cared about the optics on him and only him. Everyone under him was there to make *him* look good. It was certainly not about the team, nor was it about building up the individuals within it. Only him. And for the record, it didn't end very well for Z-man. He lasted less than a year in his role, with the rise in HR complaints and the noticeable trend of staff from his group exiting the company, leadership eventually realized he was the problem, and they took him out. Unfortunately, there were casualties, with a few of us exiting before he was eliminated. But hence the opportunity to start anew elsewhere.

I have to say he wasn't the worst of the examples I encountered, unfortunately. *She* was. Another leader who had been in her role for eight years when I arrived had a harsh style of leading. You either agreed with her or you were bullied by her. And not always in the most obvious of ways. She was not my boss, but a colleague. Though she found a way to plot and connive to get what she wanted at all costs, it was quite obvious to me, and to countless others, that her motives were self-serving. It doesn't even matter much what group or function she led; those are simply details. What mattered was the *how* she did what she did. And for that, a single image comes to mind. A bindweed. If you know, you know. This is a plant that shows up out of nowhere, slithering in between plants, climbing over them, twisting and turning over stems, completely enveloping them, creating a web of itself so it can tower over the plants and support itself. It essentially suffocates a plant, even the strongest and most thriving plant, while weaving this mesh of its vines in the most innocuous ways. In a slow but steady way, it killed the plants that supported it. And that was precisely *her* style too. So, let's call her Killer K.

Killer K had a secret weapon—information. She thrived on collecting information and weaponizing it. In the middle of a meeting, she would ask question after question, feigning interest in an update, claiming to support a project, then the next thing you know, your sponsor is pulling away, funds are mysteriously depleted, and you find yourself completely confused by not only how quickly this happened but why. The why part was easy for Killer K. If it wasn't her idea, it was destined for doom. If it didn't serve her, it was deemed useless.

Killer K operated in such a specific, conniving manner that it was quite the masterpiece. We were peers for almost a decade. We all reported to a very visionary, kind-hearted CIO. He recognized all our individual strengths and allowed ample autonomy for each of us to operate our organizations. But Killer K believed that he had to be fed information in a very specific way, so that he could *focus* on what she wanted him to. She had a consistent process; she would work to get each of us, her peers, to agree to a specific idea, then she would go to him, saying the entire team was on board with this idea or concept, and hence, he must support it fully. The truth is, most of us didn't know fully what the idea was about, nor did we care as much, but she aimed to always represent the idea as one coming from a *united front*. Killer K overpowered her boss with this strategy, appealing to the *democratic* nature and using data to paint the picture she wanted. It was tactical, it was calculated … and it was, without fail, successful.

What people learned over time is that either you were with her, supporting her ideas, or you were toast. She had a way of fabricating evidence, creating an entire storyline, up to developing a case for underperformance, then performance improvement planning (PIP), and ultimately termination. Either that or career cul-de-sac moves, where managers and leaders get dismantled, stripped of their budget, and put into rudimentary work responsibilities until they either fall into mediocrity or leave out of desperation. Sounds awful, right? It was horrifying to witness this day in, day out. Killer K was truly killer.

I can't make this story up; it happened, and I still remember it like it was yesterday. I was actively hiring for a director position in my newly structured organization when the news of an imminent freeze was delivered to us. We were asked to finalize any hiring offers by the end of the week, or the positions would be frozen. I happened to mention that I was interviewing a few internal candidates, which Killer K asked for the details about. She too was hiring for positions, including an assistant director position for project management. She knew one of the candidates; he was at that point a consultant working in her organization but had applied for a position in mine. Without sharing this with me, she sought him out, asked him to interview for her position, and on the spot offered him the position. That was the day before my scheduled interview. She tried to block him from interviewing with me, then even called our leader (he was our boss, the two of us) and claimed the whole team of my peers were not aware of the role's purpose nor had agreed to support it (so it should be paused for now). Beyond that, she went to HR to make the same claim and tried to chase the candidate around campus for an answer to her offer. Much to her displeasure, when I eventually interviewed the candidate, I was more than impressed; I was elated with his background, demeanor, and potential. I had learned of her interest in him for her role, and quite ready to make him an offer for mine; however, the head of HR recruiting insisted it wasn't my call but the candidate's. After a meeting where both of us were told the same thing—to give the best offer we had and leave the decision to the candidate—she stormed out of that office, furious at the sheer prospect of him accepting my offer, which he did. And that's when I realized I'd kicked the hornets' nest. Ever accidentally bump into a nest like that? Well, if you have, you'd know you'd be under attack in a split second and from every angle. And that was precisely what Killer K's attitude became, completely adversarial, because she didn't get what she demanded.

What was hardest to see was the amount of terror she inflicted on anyone who would disagree with her. Her words were cutting, brutal, and her shrill laugh at a failure or someone's silly idea pure evil. When she stomped around the office (because that's exactly how she walked, stomping), doors to offices would close, people would scatter, and conversations would come to a halt. No one wanted to be the next victim because there was no escaping the wrath once you were pegged next.

I remember a time when one of her direct reports, a director who we all thought was the *golden child,* the one we all expected would be next in command, fell out of grace. He had worked at the company for fifteen-plus years, had a strong reputation, and was a straight shooter with a consistent record of performing. Until something peculiar happened, and all of a sudden, he was handing in his resignation, and being carved out of every meeting, getting virtually *erased.* Rumors had it that he disagreed with her publicly and had a bull's eye on his back from that moment on.

You see, when a toxic leader is allowed to linger, given more and more rein and control, over time, you start to see that same behavior of theirs festering like a cancer. Leaders beneath them begin mimicking their behavior. Mistakes people make become fatal. Growth becomes contingent on winning favor or doing the leader's bidding.

Independent thinking, ideation, and the entire spirit of creativity completely dissipate. The culture becomes a replica of this leader's traits, just like the bindweed spreads, sprawls, and climbs all over the strongest, healthiest of plants, suffocating them, so does the toxic leader. Unfortunately, not enough organizations recognize the value of eliminating toxic leaders from their midst early enough, nor often enough, and what may have once been a healthy, thriving department or organization can gradually decay, becoming a complacent, demoralized body of resources, fearful and avoidant of all risk and innovation. This is, of course, a very sad situation, but one that is completely avoidable.

Trust and Inspire

I've been fortunate enough to see great leadership modeled before me, and I've been taking notes over the decades. One of the gifts I stumbled upon was leadership and self-help books, ranging from Dale Carnegie's classic *How to Win Friends and Influence People* to Simon Sinek's *Start with Why* to Mel Robbins's *The 5-Second Rule*. I had a habit of picking up a book that had a curious title and not putting it down until it was done and digested. Oftentimes, the author would reference other books or authors, which would then be my next read. And the next read. And recommendations from influential leaders presenting at conferences, or keynote speakers, or people I met at a roundtable. The point is, I loved to read, and I remembered the key points, the golden "nuggets" that the authors would give out of each book. One of these was Stephen M.R. Covey's *Trust & Inspire*. I met Stephen at a conference I'd attended a few years ago, where he was the keynote speaker. He was a masterful storyteller, and he shared a unique story I had heard once before from his father, the famous Stephen Covey, notable author of *The 7 Habits of Highly Effective People*. He talked about his story with his dad and the quest for the "clean and green" lawn that was entrusted to him. The moral of the story was that you had to trust a person first and then inspire them to action. If you bestowed the trust on the person, they would want to live up to that trust, make you feel that they were worth that vote of confidence. But then inspiring them—motivating them, encouraging them to act—that was the fire. The stories from that speech stay with me to this day. The vibe in the room, the movement, it was insane. What *Trust & Inspire* was ultimately about was a movement away from the traditional hierarchical mode of managing, built on titles and dictatory practices, to a more natural, human-centric mode of influencing people by trusting them and inspiring them to deliver on purpose. Wow, that was magic.

I think Stephen was spot on. You see, you can't really make someone do something consistently unless they believe in it. You can force them to do it in your presence, but once you turn away, they will stop, because they don't believe in it. That's the command-and-control way—exhausting to both sides. Leaders who have to continuously bark out orders, crack the whip, yell, chastise, and break down the spirit are using all their energy to suppress people's spirit, thereby suppressing creativity, ingenuity, and collaboration.  And the one that touches heartstrings with their words, uses stories to open the mind, and questions to engage, well, that's the one who wins. It's like rolling a rock downhill versus trying to push it uphill.

Now, to be clear, both terrific and toxic leaders put in the effort with their people, however, their intentions and their techniques are completely different. Terrific leaders recognize the power they have is there to serve the people they lead, to elevate them, shine the spotlight on them, and let them thrive. Toxic leaders recognize only their own needs and gains, using people to serve them as stepping stones for them to get ahead, and they don't care about the casualties they leave behind.

To effect the type of transformation and innovation that you may desire for your company, you have to go back to the beginning, understanding the concept of HX—human experience—and how

the approach in handling people and delivering a positive experience has a clear ripple effect on others. **You, as a leader, have the choice: You can either be a hero, elevating others, catering to the human spirit, or you can be the zero, pushing others down, killing their spirit, stifling their growth.** Choose wisely, because leadership leaves a trail, visible or not. Sometimes it shows up as fear, silence, or self-doubt. Other times, it shows up as trust, possibility, and pride. The difference isn't always in what a leader says. It's in what they *bring out of others*. And in the quiet moments that follow, that trail becomes legacy.

CHAPTER 8

The Leadership Journey

Discovering Your Superpower

We are all different; we think, feel, and experience the world differently. It then goes without saying that we must also have different ways of filtering the world and interpreting it. The way we experience the world, on a day-to-day basis, impacts how we react and the choices we make. As we gain more experience, we also gain more skill in handling situations, good ones and many not-so-good ones. The more we fine-tune the way we handle situations, the more we gain skill, and at some point, that may become our superpower. A child who grows up in a family with a lot of daily conflict may gain a strong skill in negotiating and diffusing conflict. As they enter the work world, their diplomacy and how they lean into conflict, finding win-win opportunities, may then become their superpower. The point is, through our experiences, we all have fine-tuned enough of our skills that they do become superpowers.

One of my superpowers is the ability to apply a creative, design mindset to just about anything I do. I see things very vividly, not just in their current state, but the final, polished state they're intended to be. Anything from orchestrating a Thanksgiving dinner that rivals something Martha Stewart would've crafted, to designing a service catalog that a customer may easily navigate to access and order products and services—I'm there. Part of it is because I see it as a form of art, and I love all things art. But that's me. Give me a problem or a challenge and I see an opportunity to apply my superpower in design thinking, and I'll orchestrate a solution or a new product that addresses the need there. By the way, I don't think I'm the only one with this skill; so many people have it, and few know they do, and fewer know how to tap into it well.

But tying this back to leadership, which earlier we defined simply as "influence, nothing more and nothing less," it takes a strong leader to identify strengths and superpowers in people. It also takes someone who's self-aware and can ask themselves tough questions to unearth the truth about their innate superpowers. I knew a long time ago that I love everything design, and that I had an edge over my peers when I tap into that area, creating a strategy that not only functions well but is pleasing to the spirit and soul. I know this sounds a bit woo-woo here, but it's true. *Eye appeal* is *buy appeal*. We don't gravitate to messy, sloppy, distasteful-looking products and services in general. We crave function and elegance together.

At one of the organizations I worked at, I knew we had to develop a better mechanism to communicate with our employees in IT, who were the bedrock of technological innovation. I'd spearheaded other internal electronic newsletters before, so the concept of an "e-bulletin" wasn't new. But how to do this in that specific world and how to make it impactful was the challenge. I had to assemble a team that understood the mission, that it was far greater than just sending out updates on projects and metrics on performance—it was about reconnecting our employees in IT with the mission. We called the e-bulletin *Keeping in the Know*. The concept was around not just working together but informing each other and leveraging one another's ideas to grow. An image came to mind as we were beginning the constructs of this e-bulletin: geese. Ever notice how geese fly in V-formation? Well, they do. They fly this way to gain an aerodynamic advantage with the V shape, but it takes its toll on the leader of the pack, at the center over time, hence they switch positions over time. The geese at the very end are the "quackers"; they quack to cheer the others on and to keep the momentum going. After some time, the formation shifts as the geese change positions, giving relief to others, so they can maintain the distance and speed with minimal exhaustion. I always found that a brilliant concept, rooted in Mother Nature. Geese innately know to do this to extend their flying powers, but they lean on each other as part of the recipe; no one goose can go the distance at that speed alone. So, as we formed the newsletter, we started to cherry-pick individuals with specific strengths for specific roles. The editor had a superpower all of her own—she was an English major with a unique ability to write simply and elegantly. She was assigned the writing of spotlight pieces for each edition. Another member was amazing at crunching numbers and synthesizing performance progress—he was assigned the metrics update. Yet another member had a gift in photography and video editing—we had him conduct the "get to know" interviews with staff as well as create the mini videos commemorating specific events and highlighting milestone moments. It was absolutely critical that the team work in synergy, leaning on each other's strengths to consistently produce what came to be one of the cornerstones of the culture in IT—solid communication. Over time, more sections were added, including updates on new hires, promotions, and transfers. At the point that I had exited the organization, we carried this e-bulletin through ninety-four consecutive monthly editions. All because we identified each team member's superpower and had them working their genius to contribute to a great cause.

Good leaders pay attention to unique areas of talent and allow their team members to shine in those areas. Whether it's giving them the spotlight to present at a town hall meeting, or having them do the product research and negotiation with vendors for an important solution purchase, or giving them free rein to design a virtual assistant to supplement the support channels—there are countless ways to do this. You, as a leader, just have to have an open mind and, more importantly, an open heart.

Saying Yes, Anyway

I want to pause for a moment and talk about saying yes. This is the idea of saying yes to new things, opportunities, even assignments when you have trepidation or an inclination to press the easy button, say no. I don't think anyone captured this better with a simple phrase than Nike; "Just Do It" is pure brilliance. Nike could've said "do it," to imply you need to act. But the word "just" when placed before "do it" is what makes it unique. It implies that you have hesitation, stemming from fear, or you have worries, concerns, etc. "Just Do It" says, "do it anyway, even when you're not ready." And that's the key. Most everything I've started, I wasn't quite ready for, or I was completely not ready for. I shared the example of starting as a manager of a help desk at a time when I had no prior management experience. I just did it. When you say yes to the dress, it works in mysterious ways. Saying yes to that which scares you unlocks an avenue of creativity and passion, both heavily needed to learn and gain skill. When I say creativity, I'm not just implying artistic creativity; I'm referring to the ability to think differently. When you say yes to something you don't know or don't know how to do, you give yourself permission to go find out how to do it. That's when you tap into a new world, full of exploration, trial and error, and, dare I say, fun.

Do you remember your first steps as a baby? I'm sure you don't. And I'd guess the first time you did this, you probably fell down after a few wobbly steps. But you got up anyway, likely assisted by a mom or dad, and you were encouraged to try again. You did, and you gained more confidence with each step. Over a little time, you learned how to put pressure on your feet, keep your body aligned in a way that you can move forward without falling. Essentially, you learned to walk. All because the first fall didn't turn you away from trying further. What if you approached opportunity just like that? Like it's learning to walk when you don't already know how? How you do, how fast it takes, and how many times you fall may be unknown, but the likelihood that you'll walk is high. I know it may be hard to see everything in that simple a way, but many things are just as easy as trying. Giving yourself permission to *just do it.*

I remember the first time I had to present in front of a large audience. I was a systems engineer. I know my product line well. I knew how to navigate a PowerPoint presentation. I knew how projecting to a screen worked. And I knew how to talk. But I didn't think I knew how to do all of those things all at once, and with grace. But I said yes to the role, so naturally I would have to do it. Standing in front of an audience of seasoned leaders, in an auditorium, with the lights of the projection in my eyes, the presentation behind me, and my knees shaking with fear—I remember too well the adrenaline rush that it was. But I had to breathe through it and remember to focus on what I knew and not what I didn't know. I didn't know how everything would go, but I had to trust that the only way to find out was to get to the other side of it, get it done. So, I got through the slides, breathing, explaining, using my voice, my eyes, and my hands to explain. Pausing to take in body language, ask for questions, moderate my speed based on the listeners' reactions. And when I was done, I was elated to have it over. But more elated that I was on the other side of *saying yes*, I was on the *done, check* side.

I learned over time that as leaders, **we have a responsibility to help our people get through their fears, stepping into unknown territory, and saying yes anyway. We have to help them embrace uncertainty, believe in their own powers, and recognize that learning and growing are generally not comfortable.** In fact, it's the opposite—it's very uncomfortable. But as I've said a thousand times, *you have to be comfortable with being uncomfortable.* That is exactly what we mean by using the word courage. Courage, in its purest form, is not the absence of fear; courage is acting *despite* fear. Courage is doing it anyway. Courage is the spirit and the act of applying the "just do it" whisper in your head.

Every time that I found a team member with trepidation, whether they were a direct report or someone further down in my organization, I found it necessary to make sure someone, myself directly, or someone in their circle, was challenging them to *just do it*. By having this spirit, we cultivated a culture of care and tolerance for exploration, even failure. Because there are no guarantees that when you *just do it* that it will work out perfectly. In fact, it often doesn't. But when you do it, you learn and you grow. And maybe it was good enough right there, and you moved the needle in the right direction anyway. And maybe the next time, or the time after that, it will be better, great, and eventually, amazing. All because you said yes, or someone forced you to say yes, and you went from zero to hero, not in a split second, but over time, and when it was time.

Building Trust

The word trust shows up everywhere but means different things to different people. To me, it means knowing that someone understands the importance of who you are, what you shared, and has  your back. **Trust means you're in the same boat, rowing in the same direction, heading to the same destination. It means you can count on the person or persons to be in your corner, to lift you when you need help after a fall, to be the wind in your sails when you're stagnating, and to encourage you when you are running on empty.** Bet that's a whole lot more than the simple definition you run into—"firm belief in the reliability, truth, ability, or strength of someone or something." But even that definition touches on something key— the words reliability and truth are fundamental. With reliability is the consistency, and with truth is the core *fact* or *reality*.

Earlier, I mentioned the concept of "trust and inspire," which I came across when I attended Stephen M.R. Covey's keynote on that topic a few years ago. He spoke about the importance of building trust with our people as a foundational element to unlocking people's potential, aligning them with purpose, and motivating them to action. He coupled that with the word "inspire" for a reason: People need to feel inspired, motivated to do something in order to really move with ease. Inspiration is the fuel for action. Trust is the ground beneath it. Let's say you have something heavy to carry from point A to point B. It's hard to pick it up and walk with it for a long distance, especially if the ground is not flat and you're afraid of tripping. Plus, with each step forward, the weight gets heavier over time. But imagine you weren't carrying it in your arms, you had it on a cart, and the wheels navigated the smooth ground with ease. Sure, you had to push the cart, but it isn't nearly as heavy as carrying the object solo. The smooth ground of trust and the cart of inspiration allow you to get from point A to point B with ease. That's essentially why we have to start with trust, because let's face it, if the ground you're trying to walk on is shaky or full of potholes, sinkholes, or boulders, you're not getting to point B anytime soon, or at all.

Trust, while a foundational element with leadership, it's something that takes time. You can't demand it, and you shouldn't rush it. It's the ingredient that takes the most time to develop, but then once you have it, you have to keep nurturing it constantly lest you lose it. Every time I've started a new role that required managing or leading people, I've had to work on building trust as a critical first objective. Nothing matters in what you do until you have trust. I remember a time my department was growing, and I'd been given an additional team to fold in and manage. There was a good amount of talent on that team, but also a negative, challenging personality style within many individuals on that same team. My approach was to first focus on building trust and then inspiring action.

Despite the department having a footprint over four unique campuses, I was intentional about how I approached getting to know them, coordinating meetings on site where *they* were, so I was going to *them,* listening to *their* tales of sorrow, *their* pain points, and hearing *their* recommendations on how things should be improved. I took copious notes, they felt my presence, and they felt I was listening with intention. But then I took it a step further, I invited each individual to come visit me in my office for a one-on-one, so we could get to know each other better. That team had over twenty-five individuals in total, so imagine crowding your calendar with twenty-five-plus hour-long one-on-ones. It was work, not just to coordinate, but to get through all of them, taking a few months to complete. I later learned that nothing had mattered more to them than that gesture—my time with them as individuals. Treating people as individuals who matter uniquely and giving them your most valuable possession, your time and the attention that goes with it, that's gold. I instinctually knew this, and I'm fortunate that I applied the *just do it* mindset then. Then the armor started to come off. Suddenly, the recognition of opportunities to improve were plentiful, coupled with the *how* we could do this, with a plan in motion, almost effortless once we had the purpose piece front and center.

To realign that team with the rest of the organization, I had the foresight to spend some time during one of my all-hands meetings to discuss our overarching team's "brand." I still remember the way I broached this topic, asking, "What word or words do you think others, peers and customers, would use when our department's name comes up?" What I was describing was the brand, and I wanted their honest input on how we were seen. One by one, they all started sharing the words, and before long, we had a consistent set of five words to describe our team: how they acted, how they were seen, and the attributes that were consistently displayed. Coincidentally, all of the words started with P—*passion, purpose, patience, positivity, and pride.* I have to say that if I could point back to a single moment when I could fully feel the torch of inspiration being lit for that organization, it was that moment when we coined the Five P's that spoke to our core values, and that inspired the team to align with those values in everything we did. You see, what happened in that moment was a realization that our brand defines us, and it is the way we protect the trust we build and inspire others around us to want to work with us consistently and with ease. Because we recognized that we showed up with passion, each and every day, it oozed out of us in our speech, our tone, the meetings we would have, how we crossed others in the hallways with a pep in our step—that passion was the start of the engine for our team. We knew our purpose and could articulate it at every junction—it all starts and ends with our customers' experience, it was our North Star, and we knew it. Everything had to tie back to that or it wasn't getting done. We applied ample patience in everything we did, knowing that nothing good comes easy, and we had to take others along with us on the journey to customer experience excellence. And to do that, you had to model a positive demeanor, plowing through hesitation, adversity, and negativity, so you can influence the ideal outcomes. And last, but certainly not least, pride in how we showed up, how we worked, walked, talked, and held presence in every way. The work we did as a team was outstanding as a result of this unique alignment with our core values. Individuals felt them through their bones and embraced them in everything they did. They didn't have to overthink them; it was like breathing, you just do it subconsciously. And with embracing those core values came the synergy, the flying in V-formation, like the geese, to go further and faster, rotating people and their roles through the journey.

Doing the Hard Work

I'll go back to what I started to tell you about as my superpower—the ability to creatively design just about anything. It starts with understanding the why of what you need to do and then tracing back to the what and the how. No one says it better than Simon Sinek in his book *Start with Why*. In that book, he unpacks this concept so succinctly, putting the why at the nucleus of everything we do, especially in organizational units. Without a clear why, you're herding cats. Impossible to do. Then you layer in the how you do it—the recipe, and then you end with the what you do, which is what people see, touch, and feel. You have to start from the inside and work to the outside.

What I find missing in many companies is the ability to build and sustain the trust that is required for the foundation to be rock solid. If you try to rush this, it's a failed marriage. Sure, you may enjoy the dating in the beginning, and the excitement of putting on rings, having a lavish wedding, and going on a cool honeymoon. But nothing about marriage is really that easy—it takes a ton of hard work to protect the trust you built and sustain it. Essentially, you have to do the work. And with people, it's always about doing the work, not pushing an easy button.

Leadership is hard work. It takes time to build trust, time to nurture it, time to do the things that matter most. Among those things is recognizing progress, building reward systems, and going to bat for the ones who deserve it most. That last point is potentially the hardest to do consistently. Daniel Pink's work in his book, *Drive*, where he speaks about motivation as a byproduct of giving opportunity to people for *autonomy, mastery, and purpose*, beyond a certain level of compensation, of course. Once you've taken care of the basics and people are fairly compensated, they no longer look over their shoulder for new opportunities to make up in those areas. And once you have their trust and they're inspired, the sky is the limit. I still have to say, your job is not over at that point. You have to do the work to keep them engaged, and, more importantly, champion them as they produce outstanding work. By that, I mean find the appropriate way to reward them for their effort and the results they achieve.

This piece about reward is a bit trickier than just salary increases and promotions. It goes to the root of the Platinum Rule, which we visited earlier in the book. Treating people as they want to be treated isn't big, it's *huge*. I shared examples of people who didn't want to get promoted and ones who did. Some want bigger assignments, others want time in the limelight, and yet others just want to go home at 5 p.m. and not have to worry about work until 9 a.m. the next day. Everyone is different. And your job as a leader is to work through these differences and identify how each individual is wired, so you can reward them how they want to be rewarded!

I'm going to share a little more of how I did this, in different scenarios, hopefully to further inspire you along that thinking. When I was a VP at a health care organization, I had taken care to ensure everyone who reported to me was absolutely taken care of. Salaries were at the top of the bracket, over time, and I paid close attention to the bonus structure. I knew that what they craved was the opportunity to learn, from the outside inward. Naturally, that meant giving them time outside the organization to learn from experts and peers in the industry by attending conferences. Budgeting for these became a necessary activity, and scheduling them throughout the year, a routine I had to embrace. Another team of emerging leaders needed time in front of audiences, developing their speaking skills, so we enrolled them in Toastmasters once a chapter was initiated in our organization. Other team members loved games and prizes, so we found a way to build this into our quarterly town hall meetings so there was an allotment of time to tickle that fancy. Did everyone absolutely enjoy the Hula-Hoop exercises and playing specific games? Possibly not, but the spirit was there, and there was enough fun to make it worth the time.

The thing is, not everything works 100 percent of the time. You have to keep trying new things, listening to ideas, applying them, learning and tweaking them over time. Some you keep going to and repeating, some others you abandon. With that, you learn more about your team's culture, and you build the spirit of creativity and innovation. And, more importantly, the team feels cared for and nurtured. And that matters more than anything else. Yes, on the individual level, everyone needs their compensation and benefits to kick in at the right level, but beyond that, what people need is the feeling that they matter and that you care for them. After all, this Theodore Roosevelt quote still rings so true: "People won't care how much you know, until they know how much you care."

Stepping into the Shadows

A lot of people have leadership confused with a role that gets the limelight—a lot of the attention. The truth is that leadership is about taking care of those who are in your care, as Simon Sinek would say (paraphrased). It's about empowering others to do their greatest work and then getting out of the way. True, you're not responsible for other people's success, and you can't be, but you are responsible for providing opportunity and support. That is, for sure, part of what you get to do as a leader. But not every person with a leadership title is a true leader, and some people who don't have titles are innately leaders. Leadership isn't about titles; it's about responsibility for others, putting others before yourself. Serving them. Hence, the term *servant leadership*.

But how do you actually do this, that thing called servant leadership? I've had some time to think about this. It's a bit tricky because you think that by engaging and always being in the picture with your team, you're providing support, you're *there for them*. But that isn't what they need. What they need is the space to explore and make mistakes and learn. Knowing that you've got their back, and that they won't get shafted if and when they make mistakes, is what frees them to be the best version of themselves that they can be. Why? Because we learn by doing, not by hearing or seeing alone. And we do more when we know there's support, but no one is hovering over and watching us.

I used to say this thing that made members of my team smile: "Don't tell me where the dead bodies are buried." They would chuckle when I'd raise my hand and say this. What I meant was that I didn't need to know all the gory details of everything, and it was OK for them to take action without permission, as long as they were being responsible. With that responsibility comes a tremendous amount of trust. They knew that I trusted them to think through their actions, decide what made sense, and then execute. They knew that I trusted them, and in essence, they lived up to that trust. Sometimes it was good to say that phrase anyway, to remind them of the empowerment they had. I loved seeing how their eyes would light up when they were sitting on top of a secret, something they did that they probably knew wasn't exactly right but was part of the *dead bodies buried* deal. It worked wonders that phrase. It was similar to the phrase "You can't make an omelet without cracking some eggs." And boy, did we make some omelets!

Leadership isn't easy; you have to make some very tough decisions. And as you progress through ranks in leadership, you have to loosen the reins enough and give leadership away to others. You have to dig deep into the trust that you built, allowing room for agency, executive-level decisions. And you have to be OK when things don't turn out exactly as you wanted. I'm not talking about gross negligence, nor situations where ulterior motives were at play. Just when you allow others to steer after you've guided them for some time.

Stepping into the shadows, letting others navigate, also gives you a great sense of pride. I remember when I had cemented a leadership role in my organization, a regional director, responsible for the totality of the technology suite and the relationship with the business. At first, I was the one who had visibility with the senior business leaders, attending the monthly all-hands meetings and the regional leadership councils. Until I stepped back and introduced the role for that purpose. I had to trust them to lead. They gave it their all, learning the business, building deep and strong relationships, and being present all the way. And you know the truth, I felt very proud. There was no jealousy, envy, or unease—only pride. They were not only an extension of me, but they were also the best version of leaders I could have hoped for. They were steering things in ways I hadn't imagined, and it showed. And that was one of the best ways to find myself, in the shadows of something great, far greater than I'd imagined.

Leadership is simple and so complex. It takes understanding the human and experience at a deep level, but then it requires execution. Earlier, I shared the ABCs of leadership—authenticity, boldness, and compassion. I would say there's one more thing—faith. It's what fuels the fire and helps you navigate the rough waters and weather the storm. It draws people closer to you and repels fear. Faith is what keeps you going on that long and winding leadership journey. It's also the spirit that stays with you, the intuition that helps you turn those zero moments into hero moments.

PART 3

Experience by Design: HX to CX in the Real World

CHAPTER 9

HX: The Crux of Human Experience

Every memorable experience, whether in retail, tech, or health care, shares a hidden structure. It feels effortless on the surface, but underneath, it's been carefully engineered to be simple, solid, and scalable.

Getting to Simple

You've all heard that the most valuable thing for humans is time. It's the only thing we can't truly control and can't seem to get enough of. That's also the reason why we crave simplicity. Simplicity is what gives us more time. It's what allows us to pick and choose what we do with it. It's what allows our spirit to flourish. Yet we seem to constantly be rushing to do things, stubbing our toes on routines and things that make it harder to maximize the use of our time, causing frustration and even burnout. But the ones who get this critical concept the most are the ones who gain a huge advantage in life, in dealing with the human, and in delivering HX—human experience.

A few years ago, returning from yet another conference, I came across something called "The Laws of Subtraction," a set of guiding principles that prioritize *simplicity, clarity, and impact* by removing complexity, waste, and friction from systems, processes, experiences, and communication. It was founded on the following five concepts (my paraphrasing, of course):

1. **What you take away is as important as what you add.** Subtraction reveals the essence.

2. **Simplicity is not minimalism; it's intentional clarity.** It's not about doing less *for the sake of less* but doing less to focus on *what truly matters.*

3. **Complexity confuses, simplicity scales.** Streamlined processes and designs are easier to understand, repeat, and trust.

4. **Every added step should earn its place.** If it doesn't reduce risk, improve experience, or serve a purpose, it doesn't belong.

5. **Remove friction to reveal flow.** Subtraction helps people move more smoothly through an experience.

Discovering that concept was like discovering pure gold. You see, there's a misconception that adding more means adding value. But have you heard the expression "less is more"? How can both be true? They're not. Sure, you need more value, more clarity, more consistency, more of the important things. But you also need less of what doesn't deliver all of these things. Let's take the example of a diamond. It starts out as a crystal, with an odd shape, many imperfections. Only by chiseling it down in size, removing unnecessary pieces, increasing the clarity, and magnifying its brilliance with specific cutting of angles do you get it to increase value. Leaving it alone as mined makes it relatively worthless … you may as well pick up a piece of glass.

Now let's talk about your hotel room and what works. You enter the room, and you immediately see the bed, with its crisp white sheets, fluffy pillows, and neatly tucked comforter. The two-drawer nightstands have only a single device—a lamp with built-in alarm and outlets for your devices. There's a chest of drawers with a wall-mounted flatscreen TV above it. Drapes hang to one side, and a draw stick to pull them out with. The carpet is simple, no fringe or tugs to trip on. The closet has just enough hangers for your clothes and a safe for your valuables. The ensuite bathroom functions perfectly, with a glass-enclosed shower, shampoo/conditioner/shower gel pump function, white rolled towels, a large, lighted mirror over a vanity sink, with enough drawers for your toiletries, and the toilet is tucked in its own corner, with ample toilet paper. Of course, there are other things, like a lounge chair with an ottoman for relaxing/reading, perhaps a mini kitchenette with all the basic appliances, etc. You get the picture. Aside from a few simple framed art pieces, the décor is minimal, and the space just works. There is no surplus of items for the sake of décor—everything functions, everything has a purpose. The pure lack of stuff is what makes you feel at ease, makes you feel like you can breathe. Your eyes relax and you aren't distracted by all the items you scan around the room—so you can find what you need, and use what you find, and waste no time. Conversely, the hotels that go overboard—putting in fifteen different light fixtures, which causes you to spend five minutes trying to figure out which switch works what light—can drive you insane. Some try to automate the drapes, others attempt to hide controls to declutter the space, but you go nuts looking for what you need. The point is simplicity works and has no substitute. It is the ultimate luxury.

Let's take a company we all know, Apple. From the very first iPhone in 2007, Apple made subtraction its strategy, eliminating the physical keyboard, replacing styluses with intuitive touch, and combining phone, iPod, and internet into one device. Over the next decade, it continued to strip away the unnecessary: simplifying the design, removing ports like the headphone jack, and eventually eliminating the home button altogether. Today's iPhone is nearly all screen, all gesture, and all intelligence, anticipating your needs with minimal input. At every stage, Apple's brilliance wasn't just in what it added but in what it removed, proving that the path to great experience is paved with thoughtful subtraction. It's no wonder a two-year-old can operate an iPhone! Easy peasy. Apple figured out how to mesmerize us with simplicity, allowing us to enjoy the use of the device, with no instruction manuals required, no support calls needed, and no time wasted. But the pure genius in its model wasn't just removing unnecessary buttons; it was in allowing the device to become multiple things: a phone, a music player, a calculator, a flashlight, a TV, a notepad, and on and on. I once tried to come up with the many items that I no longer need because I have just my iPhone, and it was upward of seventeen. I'm sure it's even more than that. And the beauty of all this is how simple everything is to use on the iPhone, *despite* how many more features Apple adds.

Another example of getting to simple is Amazon. Amazon began with a single product: books. But what set it apart wasn't just inventory, it was ease. From the beginning, Amazon obsessed over removing friction: no crowded shelves, no salespeople, just a clean interface and fast delivery. As it expanded from books to *everything*, it scaled simplicity alongside its catalog. They pioneered **one-click ordering**, cut out shipping fees with **Prime**, and made returns hassle-free. The **search bar** became the front door to the world's largest store; no need to browse endless menus. But perhaps Amazon's most powerful differentiator was its embrace of the **voice of the customer**. The review system gave every buyer a voice, adding transparency and trust. It didn't just inform customers, it made the experience feel more human. Amazon didn't just scale commerce. It scaled *confidence* by making it easy to buy, easy to return, and easy to trust.

But simplicity alone isn't enough; customers need to trust that what works today will work again tomorrow. That's where solid comes in.

Solid Execution

You've heard me mention *good intentions, *hit execution* in one of my earlier chapters. It's true, even those with the best of intentions can completely miss the mark if the execution is all over the place, and they overcomplicate them and underdeliver on their promises. But there are some very smart companies out there that have figured out the right formula to deliver *solid*. If you remember, I also mentioned simple, solid, and scalable as the recipe for the smile. It's not only the simple that matters; it also has to be reliable and repeatable, meaning *stability*. That's what solid means. It's knowing and experiencing the promise the same way, each time, without fail.

Solid isn't just about consistency—it's about *intentional design that makes reliability feel effortless.* For example, at Party City, the seamless experience online, in-store, and via email isn't an accident; it's the result of **systems that talk to each other**, teams that align, and processes built to be *repeatable and resilient*. When the item you viewed online is waiting for you in-store, it means inventory is synchronized. When your discount code works without issue, it means promotions are managed centrally. When every channel delivers the same clear message, it means someone ensured the playbook is followed every time. *Solid* is the foundation that makes *simple* possible. It's the behind-the-scenes discipline, the mapped workflows, shared data, and operational follow-through that turn a one-time win into a brand you can count on. Another example is **Zappos, which built its reputation not on flash but on follow-through.** What made its customer experience rock-solid wasn't bells and whistles; it was trust, earned through **every accurate shipment, every fast return, every empowered phone call.** Their agents didn't need to check with a supervisor or stick to a script; they had the autonomy to do what was right, and the systems to back them up. That kind of operational integrity, *where people are trusted, promises are kept, and service is consistent across* *the board*, is what turns a company from transactional to legendary. At Zappos, solid feels like a handshake: human, reliable, and never overpromised.

No matter how simple your solution or service is, without it being solid, you're literally on shaky ground, and in a split second, you can go from hero to zero.

Unmistakably Scalable

Up until this point, we focused on the importance of simplicity and then reliability (the solid piece). But to truly achieve maximum customer revenue, you have to scale. That means your model has to be designed in such a way that the people are in alignment with the goal, empowered to apply agency, and motivated, while the processes work with a high degree of consistency, and finally, technology enables the mass production of this service or product at a high degree of quality. The *better*, faster, cheaper mantra comes to mind for this one. But *better* is the litmus test for whether customers will continue to buy. And *better* means the whole experience from A to Z is better than the alternative, the competition.

One company that comes to mind for scalability without a doubt (again) is Amazon. What Amazon did by way of simplifying the order process (the entry point into its world), it delivered with finesse through a mastermind in order fulfillment and delivery logistics. **But the true brilliance is how it made that experience repeatable, for millions.** Every click, confirmation email, warehouse scan, and doorstep delivery is part of a tightly choreographed system designed to scale. It didn't just build a store; it built an infrastructure. One that can handle the holiday rush, next-day delivery, and spontaneous impulse buys without blinking. It's not about doing something amazing once; it's about being able to deliver that same experience *flawlessly, for anyone, anywhere, at any time.* That's scalability: not just growth, but *controlled, consistent, customer-centered growth.*

Another master class in scalability is Netflix. What began as a DVD-by-mail service transformed into a global streaming powerhouse, not just by keeping up with change, but by *designing for it.* Netflix didn't just digitize its business model; it *re-architected its entire ecosystem* to scale effortlessly. It moved from mailing physical discs to delivering high-quality streaming across continents, then evolved again, becoming a production studio, content curator, and tech innovator all in one. Its recommendation engine personalizes content for hundreds of millions, while its original programming pipeline allows it to *create, distribute, and market content at scale,* from Korean dramas to Oscar-winning films. What makes Netflix scalable isn't just technology, it's its mindset: continuously reinventing its model to meet demand, at volume, without sacrificing experience. At its best, scalability means the experience doesn't dilute, it amplifies, delivering the same joy to the millionth user as it did to the first. Scalability isn't just a growth strategy; it's how you protect the customer experience as you expand, ensuring every interaction still feels human, intentional, and true to your brand.

At the crux of any successful business lives a desire to fulfill the human need and to fulfill the desire for an excellent human experience. The formula remains the same—people crave easy, they want it *simple.* They need it to work, all the time, the same way, that's called *solid.* And finally, they need it to work one hundred times or even one thousand times, upward, downward, and inside out; that's *scalable* for you. The ones who get this formula right, most times, evolve as the heroes—they deliver what we crave, an experience we want, we pursue, and we then rave about for decades.  In short, **simple gets you started, *solid* earns trust, and scalable ensures the magic can live on, no matter how fast you grow.**

CHAPTER 10

CX: Inside & Out

Stumbling on HX

I don't know for sure how Maya Angelou came up with this genius line: "People will forget what you said, people will forget what you did, but people will never forget how you made them feel." I imagine she must've been a deeply empathetic person, and I also have to imagine she would be a fan of the Platinum Rule. I shared a good deal about how I came about learning of it and how it impacted my own transformation from manager to a better manager and eventually to a leader. What's core to this, again, is understanding human psychology and recognizing that people are the most important part of any equation. Remember that.

It then goes without saying that the fixation with customers, and specifically with customer experience, or CX, has to be around understanding what customers want and need. Companies devote a great deal of time and effort to doing research on and marketing to prospective customers—trying to figure out how to create products or services that customers would ultimately buy, and buy again. It's no secret that the goal is to earn and increase revenue, right? And giving a positive CX has to go with it because it appeals to the human desire, a major part of the equation. Clearly, people won't buy things that don't appeal to them; that goes without saying, but more than just needs, there are the *wants*. And the wants have a lot to do with the experiences. We may need food and shelter, but we want fun, and excitement, and joy. I know there are people who say they would count all these as needs, and I, too, need these. But for the purpose of simplifying this a bit, the realm of experience has more to do with what people feel as they consume a product or service, beyond the basic things that keep us alive. How you're jolted into an adrenaline rush as the roller coaster swerves and rushes down at lightning speed is a dopamine hit. You don't need that to survive, you need that to feel alive! Conversely, how your chocolate-dipped vanilla ice cream cone is meticulously swerved into a horizontal masterpiece, complete with chocolate jimmies to feed your eyes and mind well before you get the slightest taste of it—that's all intentional. It's no surprise that companies spend millions, if not billions, on researching all the different options, techniques, and nuances of appealing to all of our senses, to capitalize on the golden opportunity to give us a uniquely pleasurable CX. Why? Because that's how they get our money. They hook us with the experience. We crave the experience and pay for it handsomely when it's a positive one. And we shun it, running the other way, while wincing at the thought of it, when it's a negative one.

Think about your dental visit, the annual cleaning. Dental hygienists know that no one really looks forward to the cleaning, so they added flavoring to your dental polish, and you get to pick which one. Mint? Grape? Strawberry? Anything to improve the experience. Walk into a luxury hotel chain building recently? One step in and you're greeted with the customized aroma of the brand well before you can even see or hear anyone in the line of service. That's by design. There's a reason Sleep Number mattresses are selling like crazy—they focus on a customized experience—with a number, your number. You get to pick. It'll even come with Sleep IQ—a digital experience program that measures your heartbeat, the quality of your sleep (your tossing/turning frequency), how long you were asleep, and even the amount of time you got up and out of bed (for whatever reason). All in the name of experience. If companies are so focused on experience, because we, as humans, want this so much, then it must be the most important thing to them, right? It is. And it has been measured in many ways, for decades (if not centuries).

From my very early days, working in the accounting department, to even earlier, in my first job at the counter of Burger King, I realized that every time I interacted with people, it was a unique experience. And I say people because it wasn't just the customers that mattered, it was colleagues, bosses, and vendors too. All of them fall under the *human* umbrella.

With every new role I took and new company I worked in, I began understanding that I had to keep all of the "human" pieces in mind. The Platinum Rule was key, but then again, understanding the full human experience.

HX—The Human Experience (In and Out)

When I first started taking orders at Burger King, I experienced the widest range of customers I possibly could. The happy ones, the cranky ones, the impatient ones, and the very slow ones. People in a rush, people with kids, people with issues. And the same was true for the staff I worked with; they had all kinds of personalities. There were many "shift" managers, and I started noticing that depending on who was managing the shift, the team working was either really happy or really not. And interestingly, when the team was really happy, everything went smoothly. A spill in the aisle, no problem, we got that. A mistake in the drive-through order, on it, fixed in thirty seconds. Out of fries—no worries, they'll be right up. Everyone responded to how the manager handled the issues, with either a supportive attitude or a challenging one.

This wasn't just in fast food; it was everywhere. I started drawing this correlation in the accounting department. There were colleagues who would practically be singing when they saw some leaders walking in...and then cringing when others happened to pop into the lunchroom to grab a coffee. Why? Because some people, some leaders too, gave off a certain type of energy. It was tangible in their choice of words, their tone, their intonation, but also in how they walked, the way they tilted their head, crossed their arms, or looked at you funny. These people may not have been aware of how they created this *tension* with the staff, but they certainly did. One of those people was Z-man, whom I introduced you to much earlier. When he walked into the room, everyone cringed. And you know what else? We braced ourselves for harsh words, recoiled from them when they hit, and then lost a ton of minutes trying to regain composure or the simple will to continue working.

With every year I spent working closely with teams and individuals within them, I began learning the most important lesson about CX. It starts and ends with your employees.

EX—Employee Experience

Have you ever tried pouring coffee into a paper bag? Not recently, huh? You wouldn't. You inherently know that the bag won't hold the coffee; it simply couldn't, even if it wasn't hot coffee. The liquid would simply seep through because the paper is too weak to hold the liquid. But that's the same thing with people, your employees, if they're not treated well; they seep through your processes, and no structure can hold them or make them productive. Coffee belongs in a cup, one that is supportive, not cracked, and preferably one with a handle. The point is, your very first customers are the people who show up every day to do the work that actually produces the products or services that you then sell to customers. If they aren't feeling valued or motivated, they can't deliver to the best of their capabilities. They can deliver something, but it won't be the very best something. They can go through the motions, they can look like they're producing, but the results will be mixed. Some days better than others. And no amount of rhetoric or whip-cracking is going to fix this. Why? Because it's simple, until you touch their hearts, you can't have their hands.

I started unpacking this a while back, when I shared the lesson I learned leading the "helpless desk," trying to rush performance reviews, and realizing that I couldn't do it and get too far. I had to engage with individuals, get to know them, spend time identifying their strengths, and placing them in positions to amplify their impact in those areas of strengths. Guess what? That all takes time. *There are no shortcuts with this.* That's what separates the weak managers from the strong managers. The weak leaders from the strong leaders. There were many things I started to address, toward the goal of improving the EX of my teams, and while I'd like to say I knew exactly what I was doing, that it was intentional, the truth is it wasn't. I had to learn by trial and error. Some things worked, others didn't. But there were some very consistent themes that I learned along the way, ones that I took with me as critical elements of implementation at any position or company. Onboarding and offboarding with finesse is one of them.

Red Carpet In, Red Carpet Out

I wish I could say every time I started in a new role, I was given a warm and comfortable welcome. That would've been nice, but it wasn't true. Sure, there were some that were elegantly handled at first but rougher once you got acclimated with the role you got hired for. While others started off really rough but ended up really smooth afterward. The lesson I learned was that *everyone* deserves a *red-carpet* in. As managers, if we've identified a need for a position, and we're spending countless hours reviewing résumés, conferring with colleagues and bosses, and finally extending offers to candidates—why then aren't we giving them the hero's welcome they deserve? We saw them as not just worthy, but wanted, even chased them with a luring offer letter, but then what? They get a cardboard experience? I have heard some real horror stories about how employees were onboarded, anything from the wrong salary getting coded into their Enterprise Resource Planning (ERP) system and paycheck, to the wrong title, to not having the incumbent's position vacated prior to their arrival, to having an MIA manager on day one (and two and three of that first week). By the way, I experienced a few of those directly myself, so I know it's reality. I've also heard and seen the typical manager's first day of walking the new hire around, introducing them, taking them out to lunch, and then leaving them at a desk with no instructions for four days in a row to read the manuals or fill out forms. It's also not uncommon for weeks to go on with no equipment (computers, peripherals) and most definitely missing system access. All of this leads to a ton of frustration, and beyond that, a feeling of unease that lingers well past the first few weeks. The last thing you want to do is disenfranchise the talent you worked so hard to acquire.

What I've found works wonders is the *red carpet in* mindset. This is the approach of planning with meticulous attention to detail, the first days and weeks of your new hire, ensuring equipment and access are properly acquired *before* they set foot in the facilities, but also doing the extra work of planning meaningful meet-and-greets with colleagues, other managers, as well as scheduling tours of facilities. Over time, and with each new hire, I discovered other items that would enhance the onboarding experience, and I began developing a chart of items and timelines. At one point, when I'd evolved this with multiple iterations, I even mapped this into an electronic process for one company, so it could be easily replicated with technology forms, assigned tickets/tasks, and approvals that would allow the process to flow seamlessly. The point is, you don't need to get fancy with this; you just need to get your new hire welcomed, comfortable, and productive in as quick a timeframe as possible. They should feel elated that they've joined, just like how they felt when they got the call or letter that offered them the position. If they're starting to wonder if they'd made a mistake accepting the position or starting to figure out how long they have to stay, or worse, what it would take to find a replacement job, you've already lost.

Beyond that, while they're there, they should feel they are working on meaningful work, that they have input into how the work is done, and that they are recognized for the quality and quantity of their work. And that means that as they fall into a work "routine," that part of your routine is to keep a finger on the pulse. Regular check-ins, constant, clear, and supportive communication, and the opportunity to quickly rectify problems when they happen. And they will happen, these problems, as you know, it's destiny. We won't spend too much time on motivation now, but we'll revisit this important topic later, as it is also a key to engagement and performance, both critical to strong EX, and conversely, CX.

And despite anyone's intentions, we have to acknowledge something obvious—nothing will stay the same. It's inevitable that employees will eventually leave, either willingly or not. This could be a positive thing. Often, when an employee demonstrates strong performance, acquires new skills, and shows potential in desirable areas, they get promoted, so they leave the department but remain in the company. Alternatively, a life circumstance or a need for growth causes an employee to have to relocate and leave the company entirely, starting a new chapter somewhere else. And finally, what we never really start off anticipating is the departure of an employee through a termination, whether it's a chronic underperformance issue, or an egregious grievance or circumstance forcing their removal. In any condition, they still deserve a dignified *red carpet out* treatment.

I've never been a fan of a culture with performance reviews used as a checklist for performance. Nor have I admired the PIP—performance improvement plan—used as a weapon to torture the staff. Sure, you need to be clear and kind in how you communicate with the staff, but more importantly, you need to be consistent. No one should be shocked when they are terminated, no one. Obviously, mass terminations that are under the umbrella of layoffs or company shutdowns are different and follow a unique process. Aside from those, individuals should always know where they stand with you. There should be *no surprises*. And if and when they choose to move on to the next position, you should celebrate their move and wish them well. Nothing speaks louder to employees than seeing a manager or leader rallying to celebrate the success of a departing employee; it hits differently and shows a human connection that's deep. And this builds stronger trust and loyalty from the team members, not just to management, but to each other. The same goes with a terminated employee; their dignity should be preserved at all costs. When the communication is had, how it's delivered behind closed doors, the words and tone chosen, and the way they are permitted to gather personal items and depart with respect, it all matters. It matters a whole lot.

I remember hiring a specific gentleman as a director for a position in my department. It was a unique role, with some prickly responsibilities. The vetting process was awkward because we had gone into an alternative working style, with many individuals testing out the hybrid work mode. When that gentleman started working, he had a hard time acclimating to the team. Some of it was because the COVID-19 pandemic had hit, and everyone had scattered into remote work, and it was an entirely different onboarding experience for him. But a big part of it was the cultural fit—he simply didn't know how to communicate with others on the team and had a hard time acclimating to the company, the work responsibilities, and finally to the staff he managed. After a full year of working hard to help him transition, coaching and mentoring wherever I could, he gave his notice and opted to work elsewhere. I could've been angry, after all, I'd invested a ton of sweat, blood, and tears, but instead I opted to handle this with grace. It wasn't a good fit, and trying to pretend it was served no one. He got the red carpet out, he chose that exit, but we helped make it a smooth one by orchestrating the transition plan without unnecessary drama.

There was another time when we were being audited at our service desk operation, and one of our own had unknowingly caused a breach in security. It wasn't easy to terminate him according to protocol, and he was the nicest person you'd want answering your phone. But nice people sometimes make mistakes too. Like I mentioned before, *good intentions, *hit execution.* You have the hard but intentional conversation with them, with HR in the room as always, and you explain the situation, and you answer their questions, and you wish them well. You also have to protect their privacy. No one needs to know why they left, not the details, just the fact that they're not there. Of course, that can open things up to speculation, but over time, when the team knows and trusts you and the leadership team, they know not to push for details. Less is more on that front, for all. As long as we all remember that there's the *human* in the middle of this, and that is always going to be the North Star that guides us.

So much of the customer experience begins with what happens behind the scenes. Time and time again, we learn that when employees feel heard, seen, and supported, they show up in ways that ripple outward. And when they don't, they leak. That's why it always starts inside. The human experience isn't just a buzzword,  it's the heartbeat of your business. So, **the biggest lesson here is to take care of your people, and they'll take care of everything else.**

CHAPTER 11

The Truth about CX

It's Simple, or Else It Should Be

I always wondered who came up with the KISS acronym (keep it sweet and simple). I have no idea, and no, I don't need to research its origins or author to know that it's brilliant. Why? Because we live in a world of complexity, mountains of data, routine upon routine tripping us up, wearing us down, causing us to drown in that abyss of data. And yet, as humans, all we truly want is that which is simple. It's a human desire at the root.

And naturally, that quest for simplicity translates into everything. When we read a job description, it's because the job title was simple enough to appeal to us. We really just want the Cliff Notes version and are generally met with paragraph upon paragraph of requirements that feel more like legal language versus daily work activities. When we buy a microwave, we generally toss the thirty-page manual and try to figure out the easiest way to just get a dish heated with the fewest buttons pressed (looking at pictures). Yes, a picture is worth a thousand words, but no one really wants to *read* a thousand words to get something done. When we get a medical procedure done, and finally get that EOB—explanation of benefits—we crave understanding, and not a plethora of jargon that may as well be in Chinese and hence completely useless. Bottom line, we want simple and easy because we value our time.

Yes, I took you down the scenic route on purpose. No matter what we're doing as humans, we're generally not looking for the most complicated way to do it; in fact, it's the opposite. That's because we know time is limited, and we are mostly trying to get the best use of that time. After all, don't they say "time is money"? And if you don't have a ton of money, then you'll want to make sure you're using your time to enjoy experiences. So, when we come down to it, as humans, our HX—human experience—needs to address our wants, our needs, and in the simplest way possible.

Now let's tie this back to your first customer—your employees. They want the easiest way to get to work, the simplest way to get into the building, and get started doing the work. And naturally, they want to get instructions in ways that they can quickly understand and then translate them into action. The more jargon they have to decipher and exceptions they have to allot for, the more confused they get. The same goes with meetings; the longer a meeting goes, the more tedious it may feel, and the less likely it will be super productive in the long run (with some exceptions, I'm sure). However, smart leaders know that when they want to get engagement levels high in a meeting, setting a short and pointed *agenda* that is shared in advance will keep everyone apprised of what's to come, and drive the activity in a simple yet effective way. Of course, the quality of the communication and the leadership style of whoever is conducting the meeting have a lot to do with the outcome. Still, keeping things simple is key. That also goes for presentations. You've probably heard the phrase "death by PowerPoint," right? I know I have, and I've experienced that as well. The fifty-eight-slide PowerPoint, with each slide having seventeen bullets, including sub-bullets, small fonts, little to no meaningful imagery. Exhausting is the word that comes to mind. Why? Because it's too much, too complex, and frankly, no one can remember it all.

I remember when I first got my role as a technical consultant at a large software development company, and the majority of my activity was to present various "solutions" to companies. I was fortunate enough to get coached by one of the best, Don B., a seasoned communicator/sales coach. He spent time with us explaining the power of simplicity. He preached the *less is more* concept, focusing on quality over quantity. One main point per slide, no more than three bullets per slide, and never going over ten slides total. The point should be made with minimal words on display—you are the main focal point, not the slides. I would later learn that there's true power to keeping things at a maximum of three; veni, vidi, vici, for one, is powerful. Sweat, blood, and tears, not by accident. Just do it—Nike, mike drop. The simpler the wording, the more powerful it becomes. Now, let's take that to what it means for employees.

Starting with Why

It was always easier for me, as a sole contributor, to follow protocol once I understood the why of it all. Simply doing something just because wasn't my thing. And even when as employees we're told to do something, unless we know the why, we do something that isn't productive—we push back. Why is that? Because of what I mentioned before, we value our time and don't want to waste it. Even if we're getting paid for doing the wasteful activity. Wouldn't that mean that we crave meaning? Bingo!

This concept of feeling that what we work on is not just of some value but tangible value didn't happen overnight—it's always been there. As children, one of the most consistent questions we asked our parents, to the point of annoyance, was *why?* In fact, it may have been the most consistent question we asked about everything. In the pursuit of learning the meaning of the world around us, we asked why to attach that meaning, so we can motivate ourselves. The same holds true for employees, clearly not children, but who have the curiosity and the need to understand how the system works, so they can attach value to their work and hence, to their contributions.

When I started my role overseeing the service management office at a large health care organization, I had a big challenge on my hands. I was tasked with changing the culture of the IT team to make it more customer-centric. At the time, I didn't truly understand what that entailed, or why the CIO I reported to asked for it. Until I came to realize how mechanical many of the roles were, with employees going through the motions, but never truly understanding why the work they did mattered. That's when I realized something drastic had to happen. I decided that as long as people were distant from their customers, they didn't understand how to help them resume or improve their business workflow. I decided the only way to connect them to the *why* they did what they did was to inject them into the business space that they supported, having them go through four consecutive days of tours at multiple departments throughout several locations. They got introduced to department heads, who explained the work they did, how they used the technology, and what specific issues and delays did to the patient care experience. It was a transformative experience for the team members who, upon returning from their tour, had a completely different perspective on their work and a ton of ideas on how they could improve the way they handled customer transactions. What they came back with was energy, a sense of purpose, something they were missing before.

Before long, others in neighboring IT departments heard about the tours we were doing for my department and asked if we could include some of their team members. These included employees who had been there for years but had never gone out to the sites or seen the business in action. Over time, this became a program and eventually became part of the onboarding process for new hires. Why? Because starting with the why, showing people the why, made all the difference in the way they engaged.

The Recipe for Motivating

Once again, in my travels, I stumbled upon some golden nuggets. This time it was at another conference where a keynote speaker,

Daniel Pink, talked about *Drive*, his book centered on what motivates people; you know, what makes them *tick*. I found it absolutely fascinating and true. Turns out that beyond a certain level of income that covers the basics that one needs to survive, there are only three things that motivate employees in general. The need for autonomy, or independence; the need for mastery, or the ability to perfect a skill; and the need for purpose, or the *why North Star* behind doing something. Since these were just three things, it was easy to remember them all, and I think I rearranged them from purpose, mastery, and autonomy because the AMP acronym stuck far more than PMA. The more I thought about this, the more it rang true in everyday examples.

When I started the work to form a world-class customer experience organization (they called it the service management office), I knew that I had to get everyone in alignment behind a common why. I spent a good amount of time working with the leaders that I hired, making sure they completely understood the gravity of the impact our team would have, and how they uniquely contributed to that. I was less enamored with the words "mission" and "vision," as those were attached to company jargon that didn't quite stick much in most places. But I loved "purpose." To me, purpose was the *raison d'être* for the team, the why we exist in the first place, and the why we do what we do on a daily basis. We spent a considerable amount of time ensuring that every aspect of our strategy aligned with our purpose—to facilitate an excellent technology experience so that we can enable outstanding patient care to be delivered by our customers, who were also employees of the company. We understood innately that they needed instructions to be simple, they needed equipment and applications to be solid and free of errors, and they also needed our processes as they pivoted and grew. Eventually, as mentioned earlier, as part of an exercise we did to discover our core values, we named one of the Five P's "purpose." It was the last P, because everything had to go against that P as a litmus test to pass into activity. All the planning in the world would come to a screeching halt if we didn't align with purpose.

It was so much easier to get a team aligned and behind doing something once they knew that it was part of our purpose. And then came the fun part—mastery. I talked a bit earlier about the importance of understanding people and their strengths. Well, knowing what your employees, team members, and even colleagues are great at (their strengths) and challenging them to work in that space to *master* a deliverable, that's pure magic. It's like rolling a rock downhill versus trying to carry or push it uphill. Seriously. Think of the superheroes we learn about and enjoy watching, the Fantastic Four, for example. Each of the heroes has a unique set of superpowers, and the combined skill of all of them is what makes them *fantastic*. And that's where leadership has to identify the strength in skill, give direction, and *get the hell out of the way!* Why? Because people will naturally deliver excellent results when they're highly skilled in something, supported, and sent on a mission to deliver. They'll love to *master* the skill and demonstrate it in ways you didn't imagine.

I'll never forget the time we were forming the regional service management team, and we had some significant trust-building to do with the business community in the hospitals. It was a tall order to gain trust, build buy-in with the customer base, and begin advocating for their cause while working with internal IT teams to deliver results. I quickly recognized that I had a team of individuals with unique strengths and all were proud of delivering with excellence in that way. One director was a master communicator; he had super listening and negotiation skills, and enjoyed sitting at a table to facilitate transactions, brokering progress one conversation at a time. Another director was a master at analytics; he could sit with a problem for days, slowly but steadily untangling it and getting to the root cause, then developing a smart and speedy plan to make progress in resolving it. Yet another director loved to get into processes and map out intelligent ways to get work done;

she was a master at reducing complexity and getting to a simple yet smart way of going from point A to Z. Within their own teams, they had members with different areas of mastery, and they tapped into them regularly. Whenever I needed a deliverable facilitated, I naturally went to the one who had that skill level and would thrive in mastering it further in the delivery. Why not lean on the superheroes and let them deliver superior results? It just made sense.

And finally, letting them do it while supporting them from a distance is priceless. I learned from my early days as a sole contributor that employees don't generally want anyone on top of them while they're working. I learned they don't want the boss or even a colleague breathing down their neck. They want to do their work with as much independence, and yes, *autonomy*, as possible. Why? Because it reinforces the feeling of being valued and trusted.

No time demonstrated this more to me than when the COVID pandemic hit, and it hit our region in New York first and hardest. Overnight, we had to shift into a remote-only work mode to deliver support to thousands of employees, all in their own scatter mode. There were no precedents for this massive a change in how we worked, and with that came a lot of nervousness around productivity. The first few weeks were pure insanity while we internally had to organize to ensure we had equipment, applications, and access for everyone. Then we had to optimize the setup to ensure that every individual could hear, see, and be as effective in their role as possible. And finally, there was the letting go. We could no longer really see individuals in person, walking past their cubicles or desks, having them attend meetings in person, or witness them in action on projects in command centers. But what we had was a deep understanding that everyone was locked and loaded into their role and the work that needed to be done because they understood their purpose. Not only did they understand it but it was also their daily guide and the reason they kept improving the way they did things, despite the lack of guardrails. Allowing the team to find creative ways to do the work, to bend rules, to work in more asynchronous ways where possible gave them the feeling that they were not only trusted but also empowered. And this *empowerment,* a critical byproduct of how we managed up until that point, got extended further during that insane stretch of two years while in lockdown. While many other organizations, departments, and teams lost many of their staff due to relocation for career progression, my department specifically didn't experience the byproducts of the "great resignation." What I witnessed was that when people feel safe, protected, cared for, and can still align behind a solid purpose, they stay, and they deliver. How you cultivate that environment—your culture—well, we'll talk all about that in another chapter. That's the recipe that leaders need to know and follow to stay on the path of *trust* and *inspire.*

CHAPTER 12

Moments of Truth &
the Zero to Hero Pendulum

Defining Moments of Truth

This chapter is about the moments that matter, the high-stakes exchanges that define customer experience. Some elevate. Some unravel. And they all swing on a pendulum. I don't know exactly where I learned about the concept of "moments of truth," but I suspect it was in one of the management books I read on how to manage a help desk. It spoke to distilling sentiment from each interaction, which would reflect either positively or negatively on the relationship. In essence, every time you're interacting with someone, it's a moment of truth; you're either further building trust or you're eroding it. I know, it's really hard to initially grasp that, but isn't it true? Think of a calm conversation you're having with a loved one—your spouse, your son or daughter, a parent—it's going really well, until they bring up a topic that you're very sensitive to. Out goes the calm—you're almost instantaneously irritated—and you feel the blood pressure rising, your throat tightening, and your fight or flight instinct gets fully engaged. What next? You let 'er rip, yelling, hurling tough words, and completely changing the temperature of the room. Up until that moment, everything was fine, but from that moment on, everything changed, and not in a good way.

One specific word, one specific look, one specific sound can completely alter the mood and the vibe in the room. And the memory of that interaction stays with people—not the details of what happened, the words said, the actions, but the *feeling*. That's why these *moments of truth*, where we test each other as humans, are so important. Did you fully engage with the mailman when he told you his story about the heel injury, or were you just nodding robotically so he could give you the mail and leave? He noticed. Was the waitress coming by to check in on how your meal was going really interested in your experience, or was she pressured to get you done quickly so she could turn the table around for the next customer? When your son's coach stopped you to discuss a *sensitive situation,* were you receptive, or did you immediately get defensive and cause the interaction to get heated? Yes, everything matters, every interaction matters.

I tell you this not to overwhelm you but to set the table for what comes next. You're in control. You have the ability to manage these moments of truth, whether you're on the delivery side of a service or on the receiving end, your perspective and how you act matter. On a recent vacation with my husband, we realized the resort was falling short of our expectations in so many areas, from facilities to service to entertainment. There wasn't an area that we didn't feel disappointed in. Yet determined to make the most of the time there, we kept giving feedback to individuals in management or who could communicate the concerns. The last dinner we had was at a cliffside restaurant, beautifully set up and yet very poorly managed. The menu items were not fully accessible because they'd run out of some key ingredients, the wait staff was distracted and forgot condiments and silverware, they just seemed frazzled, and for no visible reason. As we were leaving, the manager of the restaurant asked the mechanical question, "How was your dinner?" and my body language spoke volumes. I sensed she was genuinely interested, so I told her what didn't meet our expectations. It was a moment of truth, in more ways than one. I explained things in a way that was tangible, the feelings of being rushed, of having limited options, and experiencing lower-quality food than anticipated for that establishment. Without hesitation, she asked if she could right the wrong by having us come back for the morning buffet, on the house. With some hesitation, we agreed, more to show faith than out of a desire to try them again. The point is you can have the most luxurious setting, the most amazing menu, and the most skilled chefs and still fall completely short of expectations, in fact, miserably so. Gloria was her name, and when we arrived the next morning, she more than greeted us with a smile; she actually embraced us warmly and treated us with kindness and care. What Gloria realized the evening before was that her team had failed to deliver, and she was accountable. But one mistake doesn't necessarily define you—being open to learning what went wrong and what can be done better is the way to get to excellence. The breakfast was glorious, by the way. And Gloria delivered, all the way.

Top Ten Virtues of CX

Along my travels in service management, I began recognizing some key patterns in service delivery, the things that trigger happiness and those that trigger anger. Some of it was from my own experience as a customer (on the inside as an employee, or the outside as a consumer). Much of it was through paying close attention to the *moments of truth* where the team either hit it out of the park and had a grand slam or totally struck out. I used that quick analogy for a reason. When you step up to the plate, bat in hand, eyes focused on the pitcher, you have no idea which pitch you're getting; it could be a fastball, a curveball, or…a wild pitch. You have all the skills to turn and swing to influence the hit. You may just be looking to get to first base. Or you may be looking to maneuver a double. And if you're confident and ambitious, you're hoping you hit the ball just right, with full force and lift, and it's heading for the stands, a home run. Nothing excites a crowd and a team more than a home run. Of course, a grand slam (a home run with the bases loaded) is the biggest thrill. The reality is, you have the power to choose how to hit the ball.

Here are the ten things, I call them the Ten Virtues, that make your moment of truth a *hero* moment with your customer.

1. *You remember their name.* It's not just polite, it's powerful. Using it correctly turns a transaction into a connection. It also shows that you're paying attention to the person and that you're interested in building a relationship with them.

2. *You celebrate their milestones.* Birthdays, anniversaries, launches, recoveries, remembering is caring. These gestures echo. Once you've entered a relationship, you need to cultivate it by being present when it matters most.

3. *Listen like it's your job (because it is).* By this, I would say don't just hear. Tune in. When someone feels heard, they soften, and so does the moment.

4. *Take ownership, not orders.* Hero moments begin where blame ends. The best CX pros lean in, even when it's not "theirs." And this also goes to empowerment, not waiting to get the green light to fix things—just doing it because it matters greatly—goes a long way.

5. *Follow up without being asked.* The wow isn't in the initial answer, it's in the follow-up—"Just checking in… how'd that turn out?" It's the proactive things you do to deliver the *wow* experience that everyone wants and craves.

6. *Make it easier than they expected.* The true virtue of service? Removing friction before it shows up. Simplicity is the new delight, and it's what our hearts desire.

7. *Use empathy as the default setting.* Assume positive intent. You never know what storm they're weathering so be their calm. It's true, we just don't know what the other

person went through or is going through, but if we did, we'd probably do so much more to support them. So why not act like we know and do that anyway?

8. *Speak human, not script.* No one wants to be handled. They want to be helped—with real words, real warmth. Robotic exchanges, rehearsed sentences, blank expressions—they all thwart the human spirit, weaken our bonds with each other, and dilute sincerity.

9. *Do the small thing that's actually the big thing.* Bring the charger. Walk them to the door. Forward the note. Those little things are the legacy. Some call it *going the extra mile,* but not really. It's the details that make for a smoother transaction that matter, not big gestures, but it takes being mindful to do these.

10. *End on a high note.* How the interaction ends shapes how it's remembered. Make that final moment land soft and strong. It does more than bring closure; it seals the heart and locks in the positive memory you want them to have.

So, taking the example of Gloria, the manager of one of the restaurants at this resort, she checked off many of the virtues. For one, she introduced herself and asked for my name, not just what room number I was in for the check. She paid attention to an important detail I had shared; we were there to celebrate an anniversary. Though we were almost out the exit when she asked about our dinner, she stayed and listened very closely to what I shared, hanging on every detail. Then she apologized even though it wasn't her direct mistake. She took ownership of her team's performance. She tried to right the wrong by inviting us both back for a complimentary breakfast the next morning. She said she would be there in the morning, and she was. I did find it odd that she would be working a night shift and then still be there for an early morning shift for breakfast (but perhaps she made a point to go in just to be there for us). A few minutes after we had returned to our room, someone from the restaurant delivered a tray of dessert, with the words "Happy Anniversary" written on the cake. That was a thoughtful touch. When we arrived for breakfast that morning, she actually hugged us both and said she had been thinking of us all night, hoping to see us in the morning. Wow, that blew my mind. Her smile was warm, her body language inviting, as she personally ushered us to the best table in the house. She had the servers doting on us like we were royalty, making sure everything was picture perfect, which it was. And at the end of the meal, she thanked us over and over for giving them a second chance. She made sure the bill was zeroed out and wished us safe travels and hoped we would meet again in the future. Again, above and beyond, and definitely memorable. Truthfully, the dinner was not the worst, but the breakfast experience I'll certainly remember for a long time.

Top Ten Sins of CX

I led with the top ten virtues because most days I see the glass as half full and not half empty, most days. But the reality is that there are some patterns of behavior that I call CX sins, which truly frazzle you as a customer. As I share this list, I anticipate that you'll be nodding, saying yep, been there, felt that. I know this is by no means a complete list, but it is a good one to start with.

1. *The dreaded call tree maze.* Press one for frustration. Press two for confusion. Press zero to scream into the void. The list goes on and on, and by the time you get to an agent, somehow you get *disconnected.*

2. *Playing hide and seek with customer support.* No number. No email. Just a vanishing act. If they can't find you, they can't trust you. That simple.

3. *The form that knows too much.* Mother's maiden name? Childhood pet? Just to reset a password? That's not security, it's suspicion.

4. *Fine print: the modern trapdoor.* It's all smooth sailing… until the asterisk. Then comes the fall. So much jargon, so many details *buried* in the minutiae of twelve pages of scrolling, and you know they won't read all of it. That's called *entrapment.*

5. *CAPTCHA: the psychedelic nightmare.* Find the blurry stoplights. Or the bus. Or is that a fire hydrant? Either way, you're not getting in. But you'll discover some challenges you didn't even know you had.

6. *The trial that isn't really free.* It says free. It feels like a trick. Surprise charges turn curiosity into regret. Just like that, they got you (or at least your money).

7. *Chatbots: the robotic runaround.* Looped answers. No escape hatch. It's like arguing with a vending machine. You're not winning anytime soon.

8. *Hidden fees: the ultimate betrayal.* Service fee. Processing fee. Breathing fee. Trust dies with the subtotal. Just like the *fine print.* Nothing hidden is ever fine.

9. *Robotic customer service script.* "We're sorry you feel that way." Are you? Because you sound like you're talking to *everyone,* and no one. Zero originality and zero results.

10. *Transfer purgatory (and the ultimate hang-up).* Three agents, two holds, one dropped call. That's how loyalty leaves the building.

Any of these ring a bell? Feel your blood boil thinking back to a few of these? The issue with each of these sins is that they completely discount the customer experience and underestimate how frustrated and disenamored the customer gets with these exchanges and the companies delivering them. What this speaks to is the company looking for the *easy button* for them, not for their customer. You want to make sure it's a secure portal, great, find a way to do multifactor authentication, but don't have the customer going cross-eyed trying to figure out a puzzle, answering obscure questions, and wasting their time.

One of the worst experiences I had recently was with a medical procedure I had to get scheduled. I had a suspicion that it wasn't going to be fully covered by my insurance, and so I wanted to be proactive in learning what was covered and what wasn't. I called my insurance company, and they told me to call the provider. I called the provider, and they told me to call the lab. I called the lab, and they told me to call the billing department, which then told me to call the insurance company. Each time, I had to get through a ridiculous call maze. I was placed on hold multiple times, and the call dropped twice and I got different agents and had to repeat the whole story. Several emails, several missed returned calls, and to top it all off, no answer. When I finally got the procedure done, I was out $2,500. Turns out it wasn't covered at all, and I couldn't get any financial assistance from the provider either. Perfect. There are twenty-plus points where this could've been avoided if processes were mapped properly and communication was clear and quick. Sadly, this is a simple example; there are far more severe ones, and all because the focus is *not* on delivering a great customer experience.

 **When all is said and done, people will buy products, but they will *crave experiences*.** And it's what we crave that we make the budget for, we market, and we make time to enjoy. If companies figured the truth of it all, they'd know that it starts and ends with the experience. In the end, for people, it's not about being perfect. It's about being present and in the moment that  matters most. **Every interaction holds a choice: to elevate or to erode, to humanize or to handle.** And while we may

not control every outcome, we do control how we show up. That's where the hero lives, not in the headline, but in the hinge moment when we decide to lean in, care harder, and push the pendulum toward trust.

CHAPTER 13

The Experience Recipe

Why CX Matters

The Restaurant: Cooking Up Memorable Moments

Running a restaurant during a financial crisis taught me everything I needed to know about customer experience. We had it running for four years and eventually decided that despite netting a profit, we no longer had the quality of life we yearned for, so we collapsed it. Those years in the restaurant business taught me a ton about customer experience and why it matters. You see, in the culinary world, a recipe is a well-thought-out process, meticulously crafted to deliver a delightful dish. But the whole process of welcoming, engaging and servicing a guest, from soup to nuts, varies with each customer. It can either delight them or distance them. Customer experience is a recipe we follow to understand what our customers want, anticipate their needs, and evolve with their changing tastes. Just like in cooking, the ingredients and techniques we use in crafting exceptional CX can make or break the final product.

Dining out is more than just eating; it's an experience. From the moment customers enter, the ambience (lighting, music, décor) creates the appetizer, the initial taste that sets expectations.

The service is the entrée. Attentive waitstaff who understand the menu, can make recommendations, and promptly address any concerns, are crucial. Each interaction should be like a perfectly cooked steak, well-done in terms of service, but rare in warmth and personalization.

The final course, dessert, is when the bill arrives. A seamless payment process, coupled with a genuine thank you and perhaps a small token of appreciation (like a mint or a discount for the next visit), ensures that customers leave with a delightful aftertaste.

Let me tell you a little about our business. The restaurant was called "The Nile." It was a café and grill operating seven days a week, 11 a.m. to 11 p.m. It had seating capacity for twenty and offered delivery and catering services as well. What started off originally as a *"place your order and seat yourself, eat at a table"* or *"take it to go"* concept quickly pivoted to *"we'll seat you and what would you like to order"* concept. Why did this happen? Because it's what our customers told us they wanted within the first day of opening.

You see, we had spent a considerable amount of time designing the aesthetics of the restaurant, the warm décor, the comfortable tables and seating, so much so that the customers naturally found it welcoming enough to want to stay and enjoy in-house. And we accommodated. The menu was not a paper menu; it was a personally designed masterpiece, handwritten on papyrus paper, with a painted cover. Our staff was in pleasant uniforms, and our music was upbeat and happy. All-in-all, we created an inviting environment more like a restaurant and not a fast food/pickup joint.

Once we recognized that the pivot was necessary, we invested in hiring young, attentive waitstaff to serve at the tables. We focused on training them to be great listeners, to dote on the customers, customizing each visit to their needs, and always finding a way to make the experience unique. What we heard from our guests was that they loved coming to eat at The Nile because it was "an experience" each time. They enjoyed the free pita and yogurt sauce we served to get their palates ready. The food was hot and the plates were exquisitely arranged and garnished, the taste quality was superb, and the portions always had them taking leftovers in doggie bags. My husband was a master at engagement—he found a way to be everywhere all at once, helping the chefs perfect the recipes and the plating of a dish, stocking and restocking dessert items on display while lending a hand to the cashier, and most of all, he always came out with a smile to meet the guests in person. While in business, the online platforms like Yelp and OpenTable were loaded with positive reviews recounting the uniquely crafted experiences each guest had. And most impressive, they always mentioned his name, and the lasting impression he left on them; warm, caring, and extremely generous. You see, what my husband quickly learned is that each guest was different, and paying attention to these unique needs was the advantage that we had at The Nile, which made them feel remembered and valued. Extra hot sauce, *you got it*; sampling our baklava, *no problem*; listening to your stories about the grandchildren or your upcoming surgery, *we're all ears*! It was no coincidence that our tagline became "There's no denial, you crave The Nile," and it stuck. Of course, there were consequences to this level of attention, and these included rising costs and the ability to scale (topics for another chapter or book). That's what we forget in business; every "waiter moment" is a chance to exceed expectations.

But what I quickly learned is that it's not just the food industry where this relates; the same applies to other industries like retail, hospitality, and even the airlines. Let's unpack this.

The Retail Store: Fresh Ingredients for Happy Customers

Imagine walking into your favorite retail store. The first thing that hits you is the ambience: bright lights, a clean environment, and a welcoming staff. This is the base ingredient in our CX recipe, the atmosphere. It sets the tone and makes customers feel comfortable. Some companies even create custom "scents" to entice customers to experience certain things, imagining specific places and experiencing emotions.

Now, think about the store layout. Products are organized logically, promotions are clearly displayed, and there are ample staff members ready to assist. This is our "mise en place," a French term meaning "everything in its place." Just as a chef prepares ingredients before cooking, a store must be prepped to serve its customers efficiently.

However, the real magic happens at the checkout. A friendly cashier, a seamless transaction, and perhaps even a personalized thank-you note—these are the finishing touches, akin to garnishing a dish before serving. They leave a lasting impression and keep customers coming back for more.

One such store will forever be engraved in my memory: the Thomas Pink store in New York City. The first time I was enticed to walk into this Wall Street location was when I was allured by this most pleasant, heavenly scent emanating from its open door. The aroma of the store felt crisp, clean, and by my words, like "sweet success." Each time I revisited that store, I was greeted with this fresh smell of success, and it uplifted my spirit, even if I didn't buy anything. The lights were indeed perfectly situated to accentuate each display, the colors of the shirts and ties were vibrant, with pops of color placed purposefully in unique sequences. The retail assistants were pleasant but not pushy, always within earshot of a request for assistance, and ready to complement your selections with just a couple of other items they felt would go well with your physique or that may even surprise you. Despite nothing in this store being less than a few hundred dollars, you couldn't walk out without beaming with happiness. The shirt you bought was crisply ironed, meticulously packaged, scented tissue paper, a perfectly constructed pink box to carry your shirt or item, and a matching pink bag. It's no wonder the term *la vie en rose* is used to denote seeing everything with joy and ease—and the Pink store definitely extended this feeling. While in the store, you were transported to another world, and when you left it, you knew you would have to come back.

The Hotel: Serving Comfort on a Silver Platter

Staying at a hotel should feel like a home away from home but with a touch of luxury. When guests check in, they're greeted with a warm smile and efficient service. This is our first course, setting the stage for the rest of the experience.

The room itself is the main course. It should be clean, comfortable, and equipped with all necessary amenities. But what elevates this dish to five-star status are the extras: a handwritten welcome note, lavender pillow spray, extra pillows in the closet, complimentary snacks, and the prompt resolution of any issues. These details are the secret sauce that differentiates a good stay from a memorable one.

And let's not forget the checkout process, the dessert. A smooth, hassle-free departure, perhaps with a sincere "We hope to see you again," ensures that the last taste customers are left with is a sweet one.

I experienced all of this, and more, in a lovely hotel stay in the Curio while in Portugal. The hotel was meticulous in every way. The room was not oversized, but had tall ceilings, giving the feeling of spaciousness. The décor was elevated—crisp, warm metallic accents, an insane amount of storage, and the most beautiful en suite bathroom I'd ever experienced. Every detail was designed to perfection. What's more, they went all out with the extras: two large glass bottles of chilled mineral water, a fresh fruit platter on the table, lavender pillow spray, unique facial and body treatment bottles for sampling in the bath, and a very pleasant TV/audio experience. It had remote-controlled room-dimming curtains, a very vibrant and distinct buffet experience crafted to appeal to every palate, and the cleanest facilities you could encounter—not a speck of dust or dirt in sight for miles. You know the best part of this? Not the facilities or the sleep and food experience, the people. The front-desk staff worked to be our personal concierge, helping map a daily adventure experience with all of our likes and dislikes incorporated. They understood time limits, budget constraints, and our desire for exploration and made the effort to be part of that journey. It was superb. It wasn't the most expensive hotel; however, it was the most memorable experience for all of those reasons. A masterpiece comes together when you're intentional about all the details that go into your recipe; your customers feel it in every instance.

The Airline: Flying High with Exceptional Service

Air travel can be stressful, but a great airline turns it into a pleasant journey. The check-in process is the starter; it should be quick and hassle-free, setting a positive tone for the trip.

The flight itself is the main course. Comfortable seating, attentive flight attendants, and quality in-flight entertainment make all the difference. It's like serving a perfectly balanced meal that caters to various tastes and preferences.

Finally, the landing and deboarding process is the dessert. Clear announcements, helpful staff, and efficient baggage claim ensure that passengers disembark with a sense of satisfaction and relief.

While traveling to Turkey, my family and I experienced the Turkish Airlines experience. From the warm, scented towels they offered you in your seat before takeoff, to the numerous menu items you sampled throughout your meal, to the clean and spacious restrooms equipped with scented soaps and lotions, everything was designed for our comfort. They handed us a travel bag with everything you can possibly imagine enhancing your experience; socks, slippers, eye mask, lip balm, lotion, toothbrush/paste, earphones all included. We weren't even in business class, but it felt like we were in first class all the way. Need more pillows, no problem. Midflight cravings? They've got you. Nothing was extra, and all of these things were extras. But they were not focused on collecting fees or selling product; they were focused on making your flight truly part of the experience, a delightful one. Knowing that they literally have you up in the air and that it doesn't mean your experience has to be also up in the air—well, that's brilliant. I called their experience *distinctive delight.* And till this day, if there's an option to take Turkish Airlines to my destination, I will.

The Secret Ingredient in CX: Adaptability

In all these scenarios, the secret ingredient is adaptability. Customer preferences and expectations evolve, true, but businesses must be agile enough to tweak their CX recipe accordingly. They must apply the Platinum Rule (treat people as they want to be treated) and customize service wherever possible. But that starts with being open, listening fully, and going the extra mile to give that positive experience. Whether it's enhancing menu options in restaurants, incorporating new technology in retail, offering personalized services in hotels, or improving comfort in airlines, staying ahead of  customer expectations is mission-critical. **Staying flexible and implementing change in an agile way keeps companies ahead of their competition.**

In today's competitive market, customer experience is the differentiator. It's the special ingredient that can transform a business from good to great. By treating CX as a recipe and continuously refining it, businesses can create memorable experiences that foster loyalty and drive success. In essence, you have to put on our chef hats, get into the kitchen, and start cooking up some exceptional customer experiences.

The Look, Listen, Learn Mindset

Nothing about experience design is happenstance; it's all on purpose. But the beauty of excellent experience design is that it feels natural, as if it were always there. However, that in no way means that it is easy. In fact, I would argue that getting the formula just right is probably the hardest part of service delivery. Why? Because of the people part. It's how you hardwire your staff for service excellence, and how you get to know the wants and needs of your customers so you can delight them. It also involves a ton of customization, on both sides, because of what I mentioned before, the *Platinum Rule.* That's right, treating people as they want to be treated will remain a guiding principle throughout this entire book.

To start the mindset shift within a team, you need to open the eyes of people. What this means is looking with intention. *Details matter.* Anything from the table set properly with clean linens, spotless silverware, and crumb-free chairs, to the existence of ample amounts of soap and toilet paper in airline bathrooms, to fully stocked retail store shelves, accessible to all heights of consumers … all of the details matter. It also means that when a staff member sees someone struggling, they notice and spring into action. They don't overthink the how; they learn to *just do it.* And this one is a bit hard to normalize because it requires a culture of care and a spirit of empowerment. The latter may be the harder of the two, because it means you, as leadership, need to relax control and allow there to be a feeling of agency by the staff that is closest to the customers. An example: At the restaurant, someone ordered a meal and didn't enjoy the entrée. Sure, they picked it, sure they ate it all, but allowing your server to make the decision to remove the charges or offering a different selection may mean the difference between a disgruntled guest and a delighted one. The same goes for offering discounts to sweeten a deal at the checkout counter, maybe it's a small one, but it may matter more to the consumer who's struggling to make ends meet. In the end, your employees can see what you don't—what matters to the customer—and their execution of these *little* gestures is *big.*

Next comes listening. Listening with intention makes the difference in ways you can't imagine. When a customer tells you explicitly what they don't like, what didn't go well, or what they wished you had—you pay close attention. It's not acceptable to robotically say it's not part of your service or that they shouldn't expect this. It's far more impactful to step back and evaluate. Everything is possible, maybe not exactly the way the customer asked for it, but perhaps there's a middle ground, another way you can deliver the extras. Perhaps it's tweaking a recipe to add unique marinating or sauces. Maybe it's sharing how an enhancement to the service would allow customers to access it from different venues or at different times, so it ultimately increases revenue for the company. And finally, it's seeing and hearing what customers say in writing in surveys. This one is huge. It's not just seeing the ratings, it's seeing the comments and doing something about what they said, every time. In a world where multiple-choice selections are the default setting in the survey world, we often lose effectiveness to efficiency. But the moments where someone takes the time to tell you explicitly what they *liked*, or more commonly what they *didn't like*, well, that's gold. Taking that feedback, figuring out how to implement improvements, even small ones along the recommendation, goes a long way. Even a 1 percent improvement every few weeks goes a long way. Maybe it's giving a full can of soft drink instead of pouring it over ice in a plastic cup—perhaps that's a big pet peeve of your customers. Has anyone done the math on how much it costs to buy all the plastic cups and the time/space it takes to keep an ice machine operating to see if the savings are worth frazzling the customers? Maybe the extra three ounces they get when you give them the full can outweigh whatever you thought you're saving because of the added costs that entailed.

And finally, the learning. With the spirit of empowerment that you give to your employees comes magic. When people are not only equipped to learn but asked to go out and learn about customers' wants and needs and come back to the table with ideas, it changes everything. It's as if you're turning them into mini detectives—each of them will see experience from a different lens. They'll hear comments, see body language, and notice trends that no technology will. That's part of being a human—we're masters at this because we're wired for human engagement. So why not have the team be part of the mission to capture the essence of the customer experience—the good, the bad, and the ugly—and work in a continuous improvement mindset?

While visiting a beachfront resort in the Caribbean, my experience had quite a few misses. Everything from a poorly fitted bed to lower-quality food at the on-site restaurants to the neglected beach. I kept feeling that they just didn't care about their customers' experience. But in truth, the staff cared (at least many of them), but what was missing was the *empowerment*. They were asked to strictly abide by the procedures and the protocols that they were trained on, and in so doing, they became robotic. They stopped seeing what was not quite right and failing to make it right when customers complained. But it wasn't everyone—those who were awake did try to right the wrong: a housekeeping manager personally showed up with firmer pillows and replaced the coffee machine while we were in the room; a front-desk concierge arranged for a personal roundtrip ride into town to make up for pool closures and an inaccessible beach; and a restaurant manager invited us back for a complimentary buffet breakfast to make up for the poorly cooked dishes and missing menu options. In each instance I mentioned, these were individuals who saw something, heard something, and felt something from what they learned—the human on the other side yearning for a better experience. And, with what means they had at their fingertips, they delivered. Was it perfect? No, but it was still way better than before. And perhaps when they look, listen, and learn more consistently as an organization, they'll find their way to delighting their customers without delay.

To close, by now, from these examples, you should be seeing a common thread. Everything about customer experience is *by design and not by default*. It is with intention that you should plan and execute all aspects of service delivery. It starts with your employees—their own employee experience has to matter, it has to be stellar. They have to feel valued, respected, and charged with a mission. Then they need to be hardwired to look, listen, and learn everything there is to delighting a customer. And then, the most important thing, they have to feel that they hold the keys to delivering—they have to *feel* that they make all the difference in the equation, because they do.

PART 4

Transformation: Vision, Faith, and the Ongoing Shift

CHAPTER 14

The Womanhood Experience

Toggling Toddlers and Trains

I never imagined that I'd be a mother one day, but I also never imagined a world without the traditional elements: marriage, a home, children. But there's a very big difference between expecting these elements and working with them. I'll share that I've generally been a person with strong intuition, the kind that screams so loud that it's impossible to ignore. That same intuition was what helped me say yes to the man I met at age twenty, got engaged to at twenty-one, and whom I married at twenty-two. Yes, the ripe age of twenty-two, when you really know very little about the way the world really works, but you're bright-eyed and hopeful and willing to try just about anything. That was me. Fresh out of college, planning a wedding, and starting my career, all in one year. I was smart enough to put in boundaries though; I would not rush into having kids until I'd at least enjoyed my time with my husband and gotten more settled (or nested).

At the age of twenty-five, I'd jumped in all the way with my partner, buying our first house, a fixer-upper, a powder pink split-level home, with paneling in every imaginable color, non-functioning windows, Formica kitchen cabinets, and dated sixties bathrooms. (Yes, I had both coral and aqua blue, if you can imagine this.) I share this as a bit of a backdrop for how life was for me as a young woman. I'd said yes to the dress way earlier than anyone in my peer circle and hadn't wasted much time getting settled down in a house in a solid community. With that came a strong financial responsibility for a mortgage and all the nice things that come with home ownership, a ton of bills. Still, I loved the smell of fresh-cut grass, being able to do laundry at just about any time of the day or night (even 3 a.m.), and barbecuing in my own backyard was a dream come true.

When I finally felt ready to start having babies, I knew everything would change. Exactly one month after moving into our new home, I got pregnant. I carried through the summer and fall months, with no one in my neighborhood realizing I was pregnant, up until my delivery date in February. Back then, I was still running the IT stack at my first employer, a small commercial insurance company. Let me tell you briefly about the day I delivered my first child. It was a Monday, a week earlier than my due date—it was also the go-live date of a major network conversion that I was on the hook to support, as well as the day for inventory at my husband's restaurant location, and my mother's month-end close of the accounting. Needless to say, no one was thrilled about it, and having a "textbook" delivery with no epidural or pain meds didn't make it any easier. Though it was surprising how fast everything was, I will share that it's true that you can't possibly love another creature more than your own child. No one can cause you as much physical pain and give you intense joy all within minutes of each other. And no one can look as mushy and wrinkled and yet be the most beautiful sight you've laid eyes on. The point is, love at first sight is an understatement. The bonds of motherhood start with the very first kick you feel, the excruciating pain of each contraction, and the moment you hold that warm, messy bundle in your arms for the first time.

My experience was similar to many women who were torn between the desire to stay home, to nurture this beautiful creation, and the obligation to return to work within the allotted twelve weeks of family leave. I was no different. Despite twelve intense and sleepless weeks, exhausting around-the-clock monitoring, feeding, changing, and bathing of this little bundle, I had *no choice* but to return to work to collect a paycheck. After all, there was the mortgage, and there were all these other expenses. (Boy, are diapers and baby food a hit to your budget.)

What people don't talk about is how this return to work as a new mom *actually* goes. I was nursing, so I had to work out a way to nurse before heading to work, which affected my ability to eat a meal, and if I was handing my kid over to my parents (or eventually other care providers), I had to pack a bag of necessities every day. There goes the time for personal self-care, including styling hair, applying makeup, ironing clothes. None of these is easy to do with a crying baby in the morning. By the time you finally get to the office, you're already exhausted from the morning routine. This went on for a year. When we finally had to change arrangements to using daycare as our care provider for my son, that opened up a whole other can of worms.

No one truly warns you about what introducing your perfectly healthy toddler to a cesspool of other children, watched by underpaid, inexperienced daycare workers, would wreak havoc on their health and your mental health. Within two weeks of being in daycare, he caught a cold; a week later, he started wheezing; then, a few weeks later, he got croup. In the span of ten weeks, I was going to the doctor every week for something different, giving medicine, checking for fevers, and staying up through the night to soothe my baby. I accrued many "sick days" in that time, and yet we were still expected to keep our child home and pay for the daycare service anyway. That's a double whammy. On top of the agony of caring for a sick child, the lost sleep and the cost for the useless service was a terrible combination we had to endure.

Unfortunately, it's generally the *mommy* who has to pay the steepest price. Companies back then didn't expect the dad to take on those responsibilities, so it was a disproportionate number of women who had to take a hit on their productivity. And I mean this was a hit; arriving exhausted to work, then powering through an eight-hour shift, only to rush back home and pick up a finicky baby, who wanted to nurse, further delaying the start of dinner, that was something. But then came the bathing, soothing, and story reading. Before long, you become completely unaware of what shows are on TV, what movies are playing in the theaters, and what trends are starting in the fashion world. After all, you're mostly dressed in loose sweatpants and sweatshirts/shirts most days and just hoping for clean ones. Only other moms, not just working moms, can relate to this. It's a perpetual cycle of stress that completely alters your world. No other change is this significant or irreversible.

When I eventually took on the challenging role of working as a systems engineer in the city, the intensity of my routine doubled. I had to add an extra hour and a half to the commute, and budget more time to ensure I didn't miss my train. I was preparing milk bottles, baby food, change of clothes, doing the drop-off and the pickup, as the daycare center was directly across from the train station. That was seemingly a blessing, but since I was the only mom working in the city, my son was usually plastered to the glass windows with the last caregiver each evening, waiting for mom to wave from across the platform and rush down to get him. It crushed me to see how much he missed me, and how he must've felt while waiting the whole time, each other child picked up before him. No one helps you get through that guilt, no one.

I'll never forget this one day that I had run late, and everything seemed to be going sideways. I'd stayed up late at night to wrap up my preparation for a presentation the next day, and the ripple effect it had on me was palpable. I overslept by twenty minutes, rushed the morning routine, stumbled into the daycare in a trench coat, carrying my son through the rain, with bags on both arms, barely making it before the torrential downpour. I arrived in the office twenty-five minutes later than planned, drenched, and much to my chagrin, I found my son's milk bottle in the pocket of my trench coat. I remember looking down at my shoes, with the urge to cry, but then finding out that I was wearing one black boot and one navy blue boot. A lovely sight, I had to laugh instead of cry. While my peers tried to lighten my load by setting things up, making light of the situation, I was destroyed that day. I felt so alone, I felt like a complete fool, and worst of all, I was too exhausted to fix anything. This was one of many days like that. Days you wish you could erase from your history. Days that felt like years, and tears that would start in the shower and continue on your pillow at night.

Being Wonder Woman

I never really thought about how much I was doing all the time, but I just had to keep doing it. When my second child was born, a daughter, I had to make a difficult decision. I knew what the daycare experience was like and all of the stress it brought to my household. It was not going to be financially feasible to have two children in daycare, and one of them an infant. I recall the moment my husband and I decided together that we would have to get a live-in, a nanny. One who could care for my newborn and keep an eye on a two-year-old *on the side.* Boy, was that an oversight. We hired a teenager who had worked at my husband's company restaurant and who was basically a high school diploma girl with no clear sight for college or a career, only the moment. She was sweet and kind and very accommodating. Converting the basement of my home to accommodate another person was a small sacrifice. She moved in after my twelve weeks of leave were over and adjusted well to the arrangement. What we didn't realize was that a two-year-old running rampant in the house, demanding attention, and causing chaos all day would wear down this caregiver and cause her to struggle regularly. By the time my daughter had reached eight months, she was a chunky girl with a relatively positive and happy demeanor. One day, she needed a thorough washing after she'd soiled her diaper, and the girl thought it best to use the tub to clean her. She sat her under the waterspout, after adjusting it to warm. She didn't realize my son had climbed up to the sink in the bathroom, behind her, turning on the cold water to wash his hands. In a split second, the water turned scalding hot, causing a six-inch-long injury to my daughter's thigh, barely missing her private parts. A screeching baby, and then sirens from an ambulance taking her with my husband to the nearest hospital was how neighbors described the scene to me.

You never want to get that call, the one that gives you the awful news about your child getting injured or having their life threatened in any way. This, unfortunately, was one of many such calls that I had to endure as a woman, a working woman, ridden with guilt over leaving my child to the care of a stranger. It crushed my soul to see my daughter all bandaged up from knee to the hip, eyes swollen from crying, hair matted with sweat, and completely inconsolable. She nursed for hours that day, and I once again had to take days off to care for her, and, naturally, to find a replacement for the nanny we had to immediately terminate.

I went through a stretch of five years, making makeshift arrangements with family, taking shifts with my husband to care for our two children, and eventually going through a lineup of nannies. At my last count, we ended up with ten unique arrangements to make this work, including two that were family (my father and my sister). The house felt like a zoo most days, with a stranger floating through my space, opening fridge and closet doors, displacing items, breaking glassware, and ruining many items. It was a small price to pay for keeping the kids "safe" while we both toiled through the month to basically make ends meet. The cost of a full-time nanny completely consumed every dollar we had left after paying for our mortgage and groceries, with absolutely nothing left for enjoyment. TV watching, walks in the park, and the occasional birthday or barbecue gathering with family or friends were all we had for entertainment. When I watched commercials showing a young family on vacation, enjoying the beaches abroad and dining out, I would automatically assume these were rich people, not the normal folks like us.

Those were tough years. I would wake up, set the day's agenda with the nanny, nurse my baby, shower, get dressed, and ride into the city for a ninety-minute commute, spend eight hours in heels, doing demos and presentations, and rushing to the bathroom to express milk quietly so I don't have leakage and ruin my outfit before the long commute back home. Only to start dinner, read books, run baths, and basically collapse in bed by 11 p.m. Working in an all-male office had me having to pump milk discreetly, using a white-colored sports drink bottle to store the liquid in the company fridge. I recall one day someone took interest in *cleaning* the fridge, found my supply, and assumed it was "spoiled milk" so tossed it. My heart sank, but there was nothing I could do or say as I didn't want to expose myself.

The growing years for my children had me on constant high alert. Between calls for medical emergencies like my son's appendix removal at six, his split chin accident at nine, and a barrage of soccer-related incidents, concussions, and other mishaps—I lost sense of time and reality altogether. I honestly could say there is a ten-year span in my life when I couldn't tell what shows were playing on TV (except for children's cartoons and shows), nor what singers had hits, or movies were in the theater. It was the mommyhood void. I know I'm not alone in that one, so many young mothers go through this, and fathers too, the dedicated ones who share the load with their partner. You go into pure survival mode, prioritizing the well-being and happiness of your children and doing only what's necessary. That's when the pounds add up, and your body gets pounded, literally and figuratively.

Then there was the way you felt from how you were treated when all of this was happening. My experience was that in the larger, corporate environments, there was a very cold and superficial outlook toward a working mom. A painted-on grin, accompanied by a rehearsed "I understand" when you shared a detail about a child with a fever or the latest emergency your family endured. Then you fell behind on an assignment, or missed the important meeting, and had to scramble to catch up. Some colleagues were helpful and assisted, while others simply didn't care enough to help. Sadly, I experienced this too often, and curiously, more with women colleagues than with male ones. Those who were either unmarried or without children were especially unkind, even vindictive at times, their words cutting, their stares cold, and their approach completely callous. It was as if they saw my motherhood and commitment to working at odds with one another. I couldn't be a successful worker and mother all at once, so let me leave my seat to other more "serious" people. The sabotage was real, the undermining actions tangible, and it felt like I was walking up a down escalator, most days at least.

But, as I evolved in my leadership roles, I realized that I had a superpower, empathy. I could relate to others' struggles, not in spite of being a working mom but heavily because of it. You see, there's what's in your nature and what you nurture. **Motherhood gives you both; it brings out the best (and often the worst) of your nature, and it forces you to have to nurture other humans.** I had hundreds of workers in my care over the decades of work in the corporate world; many had disabilities, psychological trauma, and life situations that you had to understand and *work with*. I couldn't always relate. No one can relate to every human's struggle; it simply isn't possible. But we can listen, with an open and kind heart, and give people the space and the support they need. I remember one day I had a supervisor who worked directly under me call me in the morning to let me know that he was drunk after partying all night at a family reunion and just wasn't going to make it in that day. I had a single mom whose daughter developed leukemia, and her life went into a complete tailspin. Another worker went from being the highest performer to the lowest, teetering on going on a performance plan, when his son was arrested and had to deal with a barrage of legal challenges to work through. The point is, life is messy, not just for you, but for everyone around you. That was the same for me as well; it was messy, and my mess was different from everyone else's mess.

I go back to the moments of serenity that I had, however few, when I would lose myself in my backyard garden, down on my knees, hands in the soil, arms scraped from branches and rose thorns, and yet those were the moments I could temporarily escape from my *responsibilities* and do something different. Tilling the ground, planting seeds, praying for growth, all of it, was how I found hope. One day I'm grimy and sweaty, nails loaded with soil and debris, and the next I'm in a tapered two-piece suit, in heels, a full face of makeup, nails long and polished, and, lest we forget, the *Hollywood hair.* From ponytail to pampered tresses, it was quite the transformation. You wouldn't believe the businesswoman in front of you would ever kneel into the bushes in that way, nor could you believe the sweaty, grimy gardener would ever transform into Wonder Woman in the span of a few hours. And that Wonder Woman, she did way more than work and garden—she cooked, baked, cleaned toilets, mopped floors, did loads of laundry every week, balanced the household budget, shuttled kids to soccer practice and Girl Scouts meetings, and read tons of Dr. Seuss books every night. She hosted the best custom birthday parties, with themes for each one, making each a memorable occasion for everyone. She also captured the moments that mattered, always whipping out a camcorder or a camera, and eventually a digital camera, and then a smartphone. Scrapbooks, photo albums, picture frames—Wonder Woman curated it all for her family.

I wasn't running for mom of the year or worker of the year; I was just trying to do my very best to be in the moment, whichever moment that was. I often felt overwhelmed, but I couldn't share those feelings with too many people outside of my partner, my immediate family, closest friends. The work world didn't have much sympathy for Wonder Woman; they didn't care what little sleep she'd had working on her laptop up past midnight, how many loads of laundry she'd done each day, or how many trains she had to chase on in heels so she wouldn't be late to work. They didn't care that she didn't have time to make a breakfast and had to eat a bagel with cream cheese bought from a coffee cart in the city, nor throbbing knees from speeding up a steep staircase in heels and a heavy laptop bag. I had to maintain my poise, smile through my challenges, lean into myself, and trust that some moments I would show up as a hero, and others, a zero. Such was life.

Loving Your Hats

I can confidently share that I have zero regrets about my decision to have children and to continue working through all of the years of my children's childhood. I didn't always feel that way; in fact, there's this thing that happens to young working moms, it's called guilt. It's a strong stomach punch that hits you in the moment you get that call about a child heading by ambulance to the hospital and you're fifty miles away, the times you do everything you can to get out of that meeting that ran late only to totally miss your son's soccer tournament, and the times you forget it's your turn to bake cupcakes for the Girl Scout troop and show up empty-handed. I can assure you, there's no shortage of guilt. Being a working woman comes with all sorts of challenges.

Over time, I gravitated to learning from books, mentors, and influential figures that it's OK to just show up as you are and *breathe.* I learned from Mel Robbins the power of the five-second habit to *jolt you* out of bed and spring you into action; from Simon Sinek the importance of *starting with why* when engaging a team; from Stephen M.R. Covey the significance of leading with *trust and empowerment* to grow. It was funny how books found me, though. One time, I was riding the two train downtown to work and witnessed a woman laughing hysterically as she was reading from a book, one I jotted down as *Nice Girls Don't Get the Corner Office.* I rushed to Barnes & Noble the same day at lunchtime to fetch the book, laughing through many chapters about the pitfalls women fall into in their careers, including baking goods to bring to the office, offering to take notes, and clearing the table after a lunch meeting. Wow. Every book was a teacher, and I took away countless lessons that stayed with me.

It took a long time for me to feel comfortable in my own skin, though, I won't lie. One time, while I was working at a large financial service company, I found myself on two conference calls, one was a bridge setup for a severity one system down that my team was managing, and the other was the Girl Scouts weekend retreat that I co-chaired. Sadly, not properly working the mute button exposed my effort to straddle both streams, and what an embarrassing moment that was for me, with a team member rushing into my office to tell me that they can hear me on the other call, so I need to *go on mute!* You cringe at those moments. And you know what? You survive them. You learn to give yourself some grace. After all, you don't wear that Wonder Woman outfit all the time; in fact, you just simply can't! You're human, and you learn that being human is the reality. This means that by default, we're imperfect.

Along the way, I got to experience aspects of the different roles that I had, the different "hats" I had to wear daily and with intensity. As a mother, I had to pivot through dealing with situations, emergencies, and balancing the children's needs with my own. As a wife, I had to find calm in the storm of demands, the constant rushing through activities to support our world, and little time to enjoy our own company. As a dutiful daughter, I stepped into caregiving, picking up pieces of the puzzle to care for two aging parents with chronic conditions and growing medical needs. As a friend, I had to be a good listener, a flexible spirit, one willing to host dinners, barbecues, and coordinate outings to open an outlet of fun and relief for my buddies. As a leader, I had to learn who my people were deep inside, what their strengths were, what their desires were, and how they needed to be motivated. As a colleague, I had to deal with competing priorities, hidden agendas, less-than-noble intentions, and polar opposite styles of working. And as an individual, I had to find peace in it all. Being present in the moment, solving the problem that arose, accepting imperfection, letting go of resentment, negativity, and simply learning from failures as they come. I also had to get better at celebrating the now, the moment I was in, closing my eyes, listening to the world around me, experiencing the varying scents, and seeing the world as vivid as it shows up. The hats were different; they were quirky and unique and fun. And truth be told, I wouldn't have had it any other way—the journey is the reward.

CHAPTER 15

The Power of Vision and Manifestation

The Tree that Inspired Me to See

I must've been about ten when I first held a paintbrush in my hand, not really knowing what to do with it. I was at an after-school program, and they took a bunch of us out to an open field with canvas sheets and some oil paints. The field had several trees, and we were planted in front of just one and asked to paint it. The instructions were simple: *"Paint the tree … what you see … all of what you see."*

Standing there, in front of a tree ten times my height and size was intimidating, but not any more intimidating than the brush that I held in my hand and that blank canvas. Oh, how that blank canvas scared me! It spoke to me daringly, issuing a challenge: "Just try." As I began looking at the tree, I surrendered to the wave of emotions that overcame me and embraced the challenge, focusing on what was ahead of me. Suddenly, the tree, which was very much alive, became more vivid. I watched as the light hit it from different angles and saw colors that danced on the leaves in the sunlight. I began seeing shadows and odd colors that I knew didn't exist, yet they showed themselves to me. It wasn't just a brown trunk and green leaves; it was multiple shades of yellow, orange, red, and hues of black and even blue in different parts. Looking with eyes wide open, I transcribed what I saw and didn't question it. Whatever the outcome, I could always say I just followed instructions and drew what I saw. After all, there wasn't a score for this.

In what felt like hours, I captured the essence of this living, breathing, growing body of nature, and was quite surprised at how deep it was. When the art instructor came around to each of us, he commented to each person individually, noting how far they'd come and what they could do to continue to capture it. Mostly, it was words of encouragement. When he came around to me, I recall a really long silence as he took in my work. As he held his chin and moved the canvas in his hand, he said what I didn't expect to hear—how it truly looked like a tree, and how amazed he was with how much detail and beauty I had captured, the depth, the dimension, and more importantly, the spirit. His words were light but powerful. The smile of encouragement and the final sentence—"Wow, looks like you're an artist!"—really moved me. Up until that moment, I had never thought of myself as talented, let alone an artist!

You see, we're all born artists; we are all born with the power of vision and to create, but something happens along the way that changes our perspective. Remember how we grew up with Crayola crayons and Play-Doh at the kitchen table? No matter what we put down on paper or molded with our little hands, our parents, teachers, and friends expressed awe and admiration. We were applauded and encouraged to do more. It didn't matter if we colored within the lines or what colors we chose to use. It didn't matter if we drew shapes, stick figures of our family members and pets, or just scribbled aimlessly … the wows of support were audible. As we grew up, things changed. We received more "guidance" to do it this way and that way. More judgment. And that changed the perspective. What was pleasurable became burdensome, and too many kids started to believe that they "just can't draw." But what would've happened if we continued to get the support to keep going, to keep trying, and to nurture this innate talent? What if instead of "T*hat's not how it should look*," we got the "*Good start, keep going, it'll keep getting better*" admonition in its place? What if those words that we use are carefully curated to lift and praise instead of to shift and shape others?

I don't remember the person who conducted this art session, not his name, his face, or his age. But I remember his words and how they made me feel. I remember believing him and feeling my heart beat with excitement. I remember feeling "gifted" and special. I remember how from that moment on, I began seeing myself as an artist, and with everything I did, I injected more of the "artistry" stroke in it. From then on, I looked at the world with different eyes, eyes that wanted to capture more than what was visible on the surface, eyes that looked at dimensions of what is there visibly and what emanates from it spiritually. That is what that tree did for me … it made me see so differently! But it's also the brilliance of the person who took me to it and who supported me with kind, encouraging words … and praise.

We are all artists, in our own way. Some of us express this artistry in things we create—whether visually with images, formations, cuisine, or even fashion. We create art with music, with scent, and with flavor. If failing at first only propelled us to learn and keep going, with more iterations, we would believe in ourselves more as the output, the art, becomes more refined, well-established, or remains raw. After all, it reflects who we are, and we are all so very different … as is every tree.

I wanted to start with this story to plant the seed about vision, and where I began my journey with seeing more clearly. It's important to recognize that it also had a lot to do with the first person who encouraged me to see everything there is to see. Having been granted that permission was like someone removing the fog in front of me, clearing the way to see in many dimensions. Imagine if we could all get that license to see with clarity and at different levels. And with that, the ability to actually see clearly comes the ability to then *imagine*.

Way later in my life, I came across the book *The Secret*, which unpacks the "law of attraction." In short, whatever you can imagine and see with clarity and confidence in your mind's eye, believing that it is real and within reach, will *manifest.* Yes, believing is seeing, not the other way around. Ever think of a person you haven't talked to in a long time, and the next moment they call you? Or you drive to a busy grocery store, hoping for a good spot near the door, and find the very first one open as if it were waiting just for you? Or you make a wish on your birthday, something you've never told anyone about, only to unwrap it as a gift right after blowing out the candles? That's the secret I learned: We all have a *power* we don't tap into nearly enough. From that day on, I realized that seeing differently wasn't just about colors on a canvas; it was about noticing possibilities where others saw limits. Years later, that same kind of vision would carry me through storms far greater than a blank canvas. It's true, this power to manifest, it exists for all of us, if only we understand it. I'll share all about that now. Starting with birthdays and cake.

Birthday Cake and Morphine

So, here's another story, and let me remind you that the word "impossible" means "I'm possible." It was a beautiful April morning, seventy degrees, not a cloud in the sky. The scent of freshly opened hyacinths and flowering trees floated through the air. It was my birthday, and everything about the day felt full of promise.

I had plans: a productive day at work in the city, dinner at Carmine's, and *Phantom of the Opera* with my family. It was all carefully thought out, how I wanted to feel, how I wanted to show up. This was going to be the year I committed to my health, to my purpose, to becoming my strongest self. Before leaving, I caught a glimpse of myself in the mirror, outfit crisp, makeup just right. I paused, took a breath, and said a quiet prayer: *Let today be memorable. Let it mark the beginning of something new.* Less than thirty seconds later, it happened. A teenage driver blew through a stop sign and, without a moment's hesitation, made a sharp left turn directly into oncoming traffic, into *my* lane. The side of his car smashed into the front of mine. I had the right of way, but it didn't matter. The impact was instant. Sudden. Violent. Metal crumpled like paper. Airbags exploded from every direction, one striking my chest, another hitting my face. The car filled with smoke and the sharp, chemical scent of airbag dust. My sternum fractured. My chest locked. I couldn't move.

At first, through the shock and disbelief, I had one absurdly practical thought: *Damn. I'm going to be late for work.* But then I tried to breathe and couldn't. Not without searing, breath-stealing pain. That's when it hit me: *I may not be going to work today ... at all.* I secretly cried for help, barely able to move to find my cell phone to call for it. The driver behind the vehicle that hit me happened to be an EMT and saw it all. He stopped immediately, came to my window, and called the ambulance. He made sure I wasn't bleeding and reassured me until help arrived. No blood, but no ability to breathe normally either. Something was clearly, deeply wrong.

On top of that, my car, a Jaguar S-type, my first-ever luxury car, was four months shy of getting paid off and now in ruins! The ambulance came fast. So did my husband. I was strapped to a stretcher, masked in oxygen, and rushed to the ER. The nurses kept asking me the same questions: my name, my birthdate. And every time I answered "April sixteenth," they'd pause. "Today?" they'd ask, thinking I was confused. But no, I wasn't. This really was my birthday. And so, I had chocolate cake with my morphine drip.

The day that I thought would mark a new beginning was unfolding in a hospital trauma bed. I couldn't laugh, couldn't cry, couldn't even turn my body. My chest screamed with every movement. I had never heard of a sternum before, let alone a fractured one, but I learned quickly: It holds your ribcage together, and every breath relies on it. There was no cast, no brace. Just time. Just pain. And just one thing I still had complete control over: my mindset.

And so, I made a choice. If I couldn't speed up my healing, I could still guide it. If I couldn't move much, I could still move forward, mentally. And I did. Within two weeks, I returned to work. Carefully, quietly, but with a new lens. That crash didn't end anything. It *refocused* everything. Exactly one year later, *to the day*, I stood on the deck of a cruise ship named *The Miracle*, celebrating a milestone birthday. The only steakhouse on board? *Nick & Nora's.* None of it felt random. It felt like affirmation. I was still here. For a reason. And it was time to do something with that clarity.

Soon after, I stepped into a new professional chapter, one that demanded transformation on every level. I wasn't just asked to improve services. I was called to shift culture. To build trust where it had been broken. To turn friction into fuel. My Hero's Journey: From the Impossible to the Incredible. I knew the work wouldn't be easy. But I had already come back from something harder. And I knew what it meant to rebuild.

That experience, of being shattered, of choosing resilience, of leading from a place of truth, became the foundation for how I  now lead transformation. **Because at the heart of every high-performing service organization are *people*, and when they feel seen, supported, and believed in, they will rise.** That's what I do now. I design transformation that starts with people. I help teams rediscover their power. I guide organizations through the impossible and show them it was possible all along. Because when you've lived through impact at full speed, you stop fearing the hard things. You *become* the spark that lights the torch.

The Tornado and the Trampoline

From that pivotal moment of my recovery, I recognized the power of mind over matter. Our ability to make things happen is real. The stronger the ability to visualize, the stronger the belief system, the more real the impact. Many call this believing in the "power of source," the power of the laws of vibration. For me, I call it believing in God. But I'll leave it there.

Now I'll fast-forward to the COVID-19 pandemic. Something we all lived through (if you're reading this in these current times), and if you didn't, consider yourself lucky. Back in 2020 during lockdown, we were all feeling incredibly isolated. My aging parents, only ten miles away, felt more like ten thousand miles away. They needed more care and attention during that painful time, so they temporarily moved in with my family while we began renovating their home to sell it and find them one closer to ours.

I remember walking the streets of my neighborhood each morning, reacquainting myself with neighbors, noticing the stork signs for newborns, the congratulatory banners for high school seniors, and the occasional for-sale sign—though not many. People weren't moving much in that crazy, fluctuating market. Most were hunkered down, frozen in place. Still, I walked and whispered a silent hope: *Couldn't one of these homes, any little old cape or ranch, be going on sale? Just one?* I walked daily during that time, savoring the last slivers of freedom, breathing in the spring air, praying for an end to the pandemic that had upended our lives. And then, in August, **something wild happened.**

A tornado hit our neighborhood in Long Island, with no warning, no build-up, just chaos. The wind was so fierce it shook the house. I was upstairs in my home office, tucked into the corner of my bedroom, facing a window that overlooked the garden, when my daughter burst in, yelling that I needed to come downstairs immediately. My heart dropped. I thought something had happened to my parents. She couldn't explain, just insisted I follow her. And when I stepped outside of the house, I walked into something that defied logic.

In the middle of our driveway, on top of my red SUV, was a full-sized trampoline. Not ours. It had been picked up by the storm from the yard of a nearby neighbor, not secured to the ground, carried fifty feet through the air, over a six-foot fence, crashing against our siding and roof, and crushing the gate before landing squarely on my car.

Within seconds, neighbors flooded in from every direction. We were all in disbelief, but instinct kicked in. Everyone worked together to stabilize the trampoline, lift it off the car, and take it apart, piece by piece, all while the winds still howled. Miraculously, there was no shattered glass. Just dents, scratches, and missing paint. At the same time, a massive maple tree in that same neighbor's yard snapped in half and fell onto the other adjacent neighbor's roof, pulling down live wires that sparked in the street. It was a surreal scene in our neighborhood. Like you were on a live set of an action movie.

And it was chaos, branches breaking windows, power lines catching fire. And yet, somehow, no one was hurt. We saw each other that day. We really saw each other. We met our neighbors in a new way, heroes, all of them, and felt the bond of community in crisis.

Now, back to the trampoline. As the dust settled and repairs began, we had to navigate the aftermath. Insurance deemed it an "act of God," so it became a no-fault claim. The neighbor with the trampoline, who'd been right there helping, shared his frustration, exhaustion, and a simple truth: they were done with New York. They were moving back to Miami. Here's the twist. That neighbor's house was right next to ours! Technically perpendicular, separated only by a corner home, and it was about to go up for sale. Quietly. Off market. He was a real estate agent. So was my husband. And behind closed doors, under the most surreal of circumstances, negotiations began. A few months later, the deal closed between two neighbors, in good faith, without ever listing the house on the market! By January, my parents moved in. And by spring, a new chapter of our lives began. We were caregivers now, with love just a few steps away.

But this story isn't just about luck or tornadoes or trampolines. It was a **true** *miracle*. Only God could've orchestrated something so specific, so strange, and so perfect at exactly the right moment. That's what I mean when I say "act of God." Not just in the insurance paperwork, but in the deepest spiritual sense. It was divine timing. A door we couldn't have planned or predicted, flung wide open by faith and force. The kind of faith that whispers even when your mind can't see the path: *Just keep walking. Just believe.* I never could've imagined how this would unfold. And yet, in my heart, I had already asked for it. Maybe not in exact words. But I *felt* what it would mean to have them nearby, I held the hope. I trusted the outcome, even when the "how" was nowhere in sight.

That's the lesson I want to leave you with. **Sometimes, we're not meant to know the details of how something will happen.** **The timing, the path, the logistics, those are up to forces far greater than us. But if we can get clear on** *what* **we want and** *why* **we want it, and hold that vision with gratitude, even before it arrives, we're more than halfway there.**

Some call it the law of attraction. Others call it manifestation. Again, I call it believing in God and his ability to *know what's in our hearts, to hear the silent prayers,* even the ones we don't know how to say out loud. *So don't wait for the "how" to make sense. Just hold onto the "why."* Let gratitude guide you. And have faith, even the kind that looks a little crazy from the outside. Because sometimes, what feels impossible is just waiting for a wild wind to carry it home. Trusting in what I couldn't see carried me through that storm, but faith alone wasn't enough; sometimes you have to climb to the edge, look down at the fear below, and jump anyway.

The Diving Board

Now I'm going to take you back further in time, to the childhood of this same little girl. And the story of the diving board. I'm looking down with trepidation at this enormous sinkhole they called a pool. I was twelve when I discovered my biggest fear, the high dive. I kept hearing the cries of my peers below me shouting (not cheering), "Just jump!" and this didn't do much to make me want to do it. You see, from up there, that water looked like it was miles away. And despite seeing others jump ahead of me and land safely (although with quite a bit of splashing), I still had my nerves rattled by the hole below. Until I closed my eyes and had to DIA—yep, do it anyway! And guess what? I survived. Turns out that *fear* really did stand for "false expectations appearing real," when, in truth, they aren't.

Till this day, when I'm struggling to do something really hard, in fact frightful, I picture myself up on that diving board—the high dive—telling myself to "do it anyway" and landing safely in the pool. It's the secret to great leadership … believing that there's a pool to land in anyway!

Let's face it: Not every task on your to-do list is exciting. Some days, the work feels monotonous, unsexy, or even pointless. But here's the truth: The most impactful results are often the ones you don't see right away. And as leaders, it's our job to inspire our teams to show up, put in the work, and *do it anyway.* The DIA mindset isn't about waiting for motivation to strike. It's about acting with purpose, even when you don't feel like it, because you trust that the payoff will come. It's about focusing on the long game. And leaders? They're wired for the long game.

John C. Maxwell famously said, "Leaders see more, and they see before." (Yes, it's true, look it up!) As a leader, you have the vision to see what's coming. You know that the mundane tasks, the late nights, and the grinding effort are laying the groundwork for something extraordinary. But your team? They might not see it yet. And yet they not only need to imagine it, but they also need to feel it with you.

That's where you come in. You're the keeper of the vision and the energy behind the movement. You can't just tell your team to "trust the process" and hope they'll stay motivated. You have to *show* them how to show up, especially on the tough days. And here's the recipe on what to do to make that happen more naturally.

How to Inspire Your Team to DIA

When you teach your team to embrace the DIA mindset, something amazing happens. They stop waiting for inspiration to strike and start building momentum on their own. They trust that their hard work today will pay off tomorrow. And they become more resilient, adaptable, and confident. They stop fearing the diving board and look forward to jumping off. Because here's the secret: when you *do the work,* even when it's not glamorous, you create the conditions for success. And as a leader, when your team sees you grinding alongside them, they'll believe in the mission and in themselves.

1. **Start with the "why":** People need to know their work matters. Connect their tasks to the bigger picture. Whether it's helping a customer, driving innovation, or setting the stage for future growth, show them the ripple effect of their efforts.

2. **Lead with vulnerability:** Let your team see that you don't *always* feel like doing the work either, but you still do it. Share your own moments of struggle and how you've learned to push through. Authenticity inspires action.

3. **Celebrate the grind:** Success isn't just the big wins; it's the small, consistent actions that pave the way. Recognize the little victories and cheer on the unsung heroes who are showing up and doing the work, day in and day out.

4. **Make it fun (when you can):** Not every task has to be a slog. Add a little lightness to the hard work. Play music during mundane meetings, throw in a joke or two, or gamify progress toward a milestone. Joy can carry people farther than you think.

So, the next time you're facing an uninspiring task, remember this: Leadership isn't about having all the answers or being the smartest person in the room. It's about showing up, doing the reps, and helping others believe that their work matters. It's about trusting that what you believe in, what you see in your mind, what you feel in your heart, not only can, but will happen. By the way, I still picture myself up on that diving board whenever life feels too high, too risky, too uncertain. Maybe you have your own version of the high dive, but the only way forward is the same: close your eyes, believe, and leap.

CHAPTER 16

The Zero to Hero Mindset Shift

Putting on Your Own Mask First

I wish I'd known the importance of self-care early on in my career, and to be honest, in my life. But I didn't. It took decades of me pounding the concrete and spreading myself too thin to see my body erode in strength, lack of rest and relaxation eliminating its ability to recharge.

What I realized most is that it's not just the physical stress of running up the stairs and chasing after a departing train, nor the plodding through the cold and damp streets of the city, nor rising at the crack of dawn to get on a plane to travel to a work-related convention that drained me. It was also the psychological warfare that I faced at times, the mind games, the highs, but mostly the lows that make work and life feel like a roller coaster.

Yet I did learn, though a bit late in the game, the value of self-care. I learned that it is not only important, but critical, to take care of oneself *first*. As a young mother, I couldn't quite provide the loving and nurturing environment for my baby when I had barely gotten two hours of sleep all night, and that made sense. As a young manager, staying up through the midnight hours to look at data and work on reports rarely yielded more productivity, just more stress. And finally, as a leader, going many months without time off and a break away from the routine, a real break with purposeful and planned enjoyment, rarely produced anything more than an anxiety-ridden environment. As I recall, it was a woman, someone whom I'd chosen to be a mentor, who first reminded me of how I'm burning myself out, and possibly draining my whole team with me. She was the one, I'll call her Kind Claire, who brought clarity to my equation. She reminded me of the airline safety rules where they instruct us that we have to put on our own mask first before attempting to help others. Imagine you're a mom on a plane that's experiencing mechanical failure, and the masks suddenly drop. Can you see putting the mask on yourself first? It seems counter-intuitive. You'd want to save your children first, right? But what if, as you're messing with the tangled masks, you pass out—and you save neither your kids nor yourself. That's why you put on your mask first, so you're equipped to save the others.

So, the lesson I learned over time was that self-care is essential. It's good for the mind, the body, and the soul. Whether it's leaving at a reasonable work end time and allowing yourself the nap on the train, or it's the purposeful scheduling of a massage or a manicure, or it's the decision to eat out versus toiling for hours to prepare a meal after a very long day—it's all part of it. It's also the deliberate planning of downtime to enjoy. Yes, actually planning how to bring joy into your world. That will mean different things to different people. It's a vacation from the day-to-day responsibilities, and sometimes it means going away and exploring different parts of the world, but many times it's just allowing yourself to do the things that make you happy. You escape from responsibility to others and tend to your responsibility to yourself—taking care of you.

For me, I've found that joy in a few places: the garden and all that it offers by way of hope and the promise of beauty and bounty; the beach and its constant soothing and healing rhythm; and sur-prisingly, the kitchen, where I get to unlock a world of sensory sat-isfaction via baking and cooking. I have also been more deliberate with planning of vacations, sometimes for basic basking in the sun, but most times for exploring and charting new courses around unique venues through the world, capturing as many moments as possible via photos and videos, is a huge passion of mine.

The important thing to remember here is that *how* you care for yourself is up to you, as long as you understand the importance of the *why* and are consistent with the *when* it's needed. As they say, *you can't pour out of an empty cup,* so step number one, always be filling your own cup. So be intentional with self-care, plan it, make it happen, and never be apologetic about it. You'll find that if you do, in fact, neglect this area, putting yourself last, you'll turn many of life's moments from hero moments to zero moments.

Open Heart, Open Mind

Going back to the key to transformation is your mindset. Understanding that to truly impact people, you have to be open with both your heart and your mind. That means assuming that people generally have positive intent. Imagine if you could start from that point, knowing that people have good intentions (and often just *hit execution) just the same. Obviously, we can't read people's minds, so we don't always know what their intentions are, but if we were to look at their actions through the lens of good intention, that would really change things. I know we tend to do that with the people we know and love the most; we *cut them a lot of slack.* Why do we do that? Because we know them to be good at heart, and even when they don't execute well, we're more kind and forgiving of them. But that's also true for humans in general. Everyone's just trying to do the best with what they have. Not everyone has it easy, and we don't truly know what someone may be going through. Though we're not therapists, equipped to unpack the trauma a person may have and the reason why they are acting/reacting in a certain way, we still have the capacity to be kind and compassionate. Assuming they have good reason to act in a certain way—hardships we don't understand, experiences that are unfamiliar to us—helps us give them space and act toward them with grace.

I would say it doesn't even matter what side of the equation this is on. Whether you're a leader guiding a team or a customer *experiencing* a service, think of the person or people you're dealing with, and prioritize the human, the HX (human experience), in that interaction. Remember, every contact with a person is a moment of truth, and how you interact, communicate, and yes, give grace, turns those moments into hero moments and far fewer zero moments.

Look, Listen, Learn

Back in the late 1960s into 1970, there was an educational show called *Look, Listen and Learn.* It aired for only one or two years and focused on opening the mind to learning by prioritizing deep vision and listening skills. I don't know quite why that stayed with me through all these years, though I suspect the series played at a time my babysitter plopped me in front of the TV on a regular basis, so I must've liked something about it.

Over time, I'd come back to the power of vision, as I unpacked that a few chapters back when I shared the story of the *tree that inspired me to see.* Looking at something with blank eyes is not the same as looking at it with intention. The way I was instructed to look at the tree, seeing the shape, the colors, the shadows, the texture, all of that mattered. It was the instruction that helped guide me to seeing, and then the encouragement to put that into practice by painting it. The same holds true with people and especially with service. You want to see things firsthand, how people interact with a service or product, what selections they make, what time it takes, how they react to steps in the process. You can see their sentiment, especially by observing their body language. So, I would say that learning how to watch body language and interpret it is an important skill to acquire.

The other thing that goes with looking and interpreting what you see is *what you hear*. You see what you hear is not just the *audible words* that are spoken, it's the *voice sound* levels, the *pitch*, the intonation, and the speed. How short or long the sentences are, the speed with which someone is talking, the way they raise or lower their voice, and even their choice of words. All of it is a colorful kaleidoscope of meaning to interpret. In addition, it's what isn't said that can often matter more than what's said. We call this *reading between the lines*. Listening with the intention to understand is a powerful skill, and one that is grossly underestimated in its importance. I would argue that it is one of the skills most lacking in today's workforce and home environments. But learning to fine-tune this skill takes a lot of patience and practice. It entails not only waiting for people to fully complete their sentences, but it also means asking questions to gain clarity and to show that you understand their meaning. Yes, good listening is hard to do. We generally make the mistake of listening with the intent to respond and not the intent to understand. And that's where friction comes in. So many arguments and conflicts arise when we don't actually understand the person because we weren't actively listening. Or we were doing surface-level listening without validating understanding and intent.

What I learned to do over time was use specific phrases like, "Let me make sure I understand what you're trying to tell me" (and then repeat back a version of what they said in my own words). I also would use questions like "tell me more about …" and "help me understand this concept, I'm not quite there …" and lastly, when I heard and understood but didn't agree, "I hear you, and I understand what you're saying. I see things a bit differently …" (then sharing an alternative view).

The goal of looking, listening, and learning with an open heart and mind is one thing—to learn. When we learn about the people, the why they do what they do, then we can be present and more helpful to them. Learning helps us honor the person and be more effective in the human experience, the transaction we're trying to facilitate. In earlier chapters, I shared many examples of how I learned to learn about the people I worked with. Some of it was rough, some of it was smooth. It takes time to fine-tune that skill of learning, but as long as you're curious and prioritize the human experience, you'll find you're drawn to it more naturally, and you can fine-tune your skill with time. The best leaders are lifelong learners. And I have to remind you, they look at the world through the lens of a gardener, learning what every person, like every plant, needs to grow and thrive. That also goes back to the Platinum Rule—treating people as they want to be treated. Just like in a garden, you can't tend to all the plants in exactly the same way; you have to understand their wants and needs, set up the best environment to nurture and maintain their growth, and lastly, be consistent in providing that nurturing environment.

Believing

I want to end on this positive note—believing is seeing. It's contrary to the old saying "seeing is believing," which goes off the premise that once you see something, you have proof of its existence, so you believe in it. That's an *if-then* scenario. But what if you can rewire your thinking to imagine the possibility, in your mind's eye, seeing, hearing, smelling, tasting, and feeling something? Can you do it? Imagine a bright yellow lemon sitting on your counter. You can see its bumpy, rubbery skin, the pores on the peel, and with a sharp knife you use to cut it in half, you can see the juicy pulp and the veins and the seeds on the inside. You hear the sound of the knife slicing smoothly through the skin and into the core of the lemon. Then you get a whiff of the powerful scent of the lemon as it travels up to your nose. Suddenly, your taste buds start to react in anticipation of the sour, tart flavor of a slice of this lemon as you lift it to your mouth. With your fingers, you feel the texture of the slice, the coldness of the lemon, and the sting of the liquid as it runs down your fingers, finding a small cut between your thumb and forefinger, and suddenly you wince! I've just taken you through a short journey of exploring all five senses, simply using your mind. None of this really happened, but in your mind, it did.

You have the power to manifest your own reality, one moment at a time. Whatever you can see happening, feeling it, appreciating it, you can make happen. I truly believe this, and I want you to believe it too. Too many people sabotage themselves by constantly thinking in the negative, allowing supposed *reality check* questions and dialogues to live in their brains. I *can't do* this, and I can't do that. This simply can't be, it's not for me. If you keep thinking and feeling that way, it's exactly how it will be. Henry Ford said it best, "Whether you think you can, or you think you can't, you're right." Harnessing the power of your mind is the first step to manifesting your desires.

I'll leave you with a few final thoughts. Your mind is a garden, your thoughts are the seeds, you can plant flowers, or you can plant weeds. Don't know who to credit this saying to, but the important thing is the connection between thoughts and actions. I also like this other admonition: "Watch your thoughts, for they become your words. Watch your words, for they become your actions. Watch your actions, for they become your habits. Watch your habits, for they become your character. Watch your character, for it becomes your destiny." This too is a quote I can't quite attribute to a person, though its power is unmistakable—tying thoughts to destiny through this unique relationship sequence. The power of thought and vision is undeniable. I shared many stories and lessons in this book to give you a perspective rooted in real-world experience, hoping this helps dislodge some limiting beliefs and open up a channel to experience the world differently. Again, every interaction with a human (a customer too) is a moment of truth. They can be zero moments or they can be hero moments. It's all up to you, it's true. You have the power; the choice is ultimately yours.

This book began with my story, but it was never just about me. It was always about you. The lessons, the mistakes, the triumphs, they are reminders that we are all works in progress, always refining, never fully finished. The zero-to-hero journey isn't a single leap; it is a choice made again and again, to believe in yourself, to care for yourself, to open your heart, and to keep learning. Now the pen is in your hand. You've read my journey, you've seen my pivots, but your story is still being written. Choose self-care as your oxygen. Choose compassion and curiosity as your fuel. Choose to look, listen, and learn before you act. And above all, choose to believe in yourself, in others, and in the unseen possibilities ahead. If you do, you won't just find hero moments. You will create them. And that is where your story begins.

ACKNOWLEDGMENTS

This book has been a labor of heart and soul. It is a collection of lessons, stories, and truths gathered over years of experience—not just my own, but those generously shared by others who shaped me along the way. I have poured myself into these pages because I wanted to give back some of the wisdom I have been given, the kind that is earned through trial, triumph, and transformation.

So many people have participated in this journey, some by inspiring me to grow, others by showing me what to avoid. I am grateful for them all. Every lesson, good or bad, made the themes in this book clearer, more grounded, and more human. I hope readers will gain as much from these reflections as I did from living them. I truly believe that people are good on the inside, that they want to be kind, present, and helpful. Sometimes we just need to remind each other how.

To my family, you are my foundation:

To my mother, the greatest influence in my life. She was a pillar of strength and modeled humanity and empathy in a way few ever could. She taught me the power of assuming positive intent and the peace that comes with letting things go.

To my father, who taught me to speak clearly and with conviction, to believe in the power of hard work, and to always keep my word.

To my husband, who reminds me every day that service to others is its own reward.

To my children, who continually teach me to be present, to find joy in the big and little things, and to nurture creativity as a family value.

And to my siblings, who taught me what it means to be responsible, to capture life's moments, and to find joy in gathering and celebrating in our own quirky ways. You are the strength we lean on in one another, and I am forever grateful for the bond we share.

To my friends, the constants through every chapter of life:

To the childhood besties who have known me the longest, the beautifully crazy ones who remind me to laugh louder, and the newer friends who entered my world just when I needed them most. Each of you has brought light, joy, and balance to my journey. You were not here for a season, but for a reason, and I am deeply grateful for the memories, support, and love we continue to share.

To my coaches, I am grateful for your guidance and belief:

Ken, who helped me see the full breadth of my skills and guided me as I shaped my personal brand.

Jen, who challenged me to think big, build meaningful connections, and design a system that supports my entrepreneurial path.

To my mentors, your wisdom reshaped my thinking:

Rob, who listened deeply, provided wisdom and guidance, and helped me believe in my own potential.

Sam, who helped me recognize the power of my voice and the depth of my influence, so I could embrace my uniqueness.

Clarice and Lisa, who shared their insights on entrepreneurship and the unpredictable art of corporate life.

**To my sponsors, thank you for opening doors
and believing before I did:**

Denise, the first to give me a chance, even vacating her own seat so I could step into my first technical role.

Rob, who saw leadership potential in me, challenged me to lead and not just manage, and opened many doors of opportunity for me.

Jack, who gave me a blank slate, empowered me to execute a complete transformation, and inspired me to raise other leaders along the way.

To my teams and peers, you made the work worthwhile:

To my brothers from CA, thank you for being the camaraderie and support I needed when I was young and inexperienced in IT.

To my service management team from Monte, you made me proud to be a servant leader and reminded me daily of what it means to lead with heart.

And to my colleagues who graciously accepted my invitation to read this book before its release, thank you for taking a chance on an untold story, and for offering thoughtful feedback and heartfelt testimonials when it moved you.

To the thought leaders who shaped my thinking, your words lit the path:

Dale Carnegie, for showing me that kindness and influence go hand in hand.

John C. Maxwell, for teaching what leadership truly is and what it is not.

Simon Sinek, for helping me rediscover purpose and starting with "why."

Brené Brown, for reminding me that clear is kind and that vulnerability is strength.

Stephen M. R. Covey, for proving that trust and inspiration can outshine command and control.

And Mel Robbins, for the five-second push I did not know I needed, and for inspiring me weekly to keep moving forward.

To everyone who has crossed my path, thank you for the lessons, the grace, and the growth. You have each left fingerprints on this journey.

At its core, this book is about the human experience, the small moments that shape us, the choices that reveal us, and the courage it takes to keep showing up. Thank you for being part of mine.

YOUR NOTES